THE BARUCH PAPERS

A journal of articles to bring a timely word spoken in due season.

Introduction

Baruch was a scribe for the prophet Jeremiah, entrusted to write down all the words that Jeremiah received from the Lord. Baruch wrote on a scroll all the words prophesied by Jeremiah and then took the scroll with the words God spoke through Jeremiah and read them within the hearing of God's people at the temple.

There are spiritual truths and insights that God has for His people that are timely for 2024. They are words to encourage, teach, develop, strengthen, and prepare us for the year ahead. Enclosed in this Journal are 12 articles written by men and women of God. These are articles written to bring His timely Word to those who are open and excited to hear. They are to bring life from His Word for the year ahead, just as Proverbs 15:23 refers to "…a word spoken in due season, how good it is."

Each journal author was free to listen to the Holy Spirit and write as the Lord led them. In this manner, they are like the man, Baruch, for whom this Journal was titled. And, like Baruch, they have acted as a scribe by listening and then writing the Word the Lord has given them. Then, just as Baruch was instructed to read those words within the hearing of God's people, the authors have shared these Words with each of us.

There is no attempt to present a uniform message, only to "awaken our ears to hear as the learned," as Isaiah said. With that in mind, we are pleased and excited to present to you a timely word in due season, the season of 2024.

Special Thanks

A heartfelt thanks to all of our authors for seeking God for a word to share about the year to come, 2024.

A special thank you and much gratitude, to our good friend, Dianne Sitter, for volunteering to edit this collection of articles for us.

May all of us seek the Holy Spirit for His personal word fur us as individuals as we enter 2024.

"The law and the prophets were until John. Since that time the kingdom of God has been preached, and everyone is pressing into it." Luke 16:16 NKJV

Table of Contents

Lonely By Myself: Gospel Hope For An Epidemic Of Loneliness

By Pastor Tommy Briggs

It's such a lonely life,
I almost cry each night,
Cause fate has put me on the shelf.
I get so lonely, so lonely by myself.

- Larry Norman
Lonely By Myself

In early 2023, U.S. Surgeon General Dr. Vivek H. Murthy released a shocking report entitled *Our Epidemic of Loneliness and Isolation*. In it, he detailed how loneliness among Americans has reached epidemic levels, noting that "approximately half of U.S. adults report experiencing loneliness." Rates of loneliness among young people are even higher, with "young adults . . . almost twice as likely to report feeling lonely than those over 65. The rate of loneliness among young adults has increased every year between 1976 and 2019." This sad trend is not limited to America. ABC RN, citing a survey by the "men's health organization Healthy Male, found that 43 percent of Australian men were lonely, with 16 percent experiencing high levels of loneliness." The Center for Bible Engagement conducted a study among people of various faiths around the world. Among the findings were that 49% of Buddhists, 46% of Chinese Traditionalists, 52% of Hindus, 34% of Jews, and 46% of Muslims all struggle with loneliness on a regular basis. Christians are not immune to this trend. A 2020 Barna Group poll found that 1 in 5 Christians reported feeling lonely.

This trend has been exacerbated by many factors, one of the main ones being the nature of new technologies. Social media and smartphones have come to monopolize our daily interactions. According to the Surgeon General, "Americans spend an average of six hours per day on digital media. One-in-three U.S. adults 18 and over report that they are online 'almost constantly,' and the percentage of teens ages 13 to 17 who say they are online 'almost constantly' has doubled since 2015." This heavy online engagement has been directly linked to negative social outcomes. "In a U.S.-based study, participants who reported using social media for more than two hours a day had about double the odds of reporting increased perceptions of social isolation compared to those who used social media for less than 30 minutes per day." Arnie Cole of the Center for Bible Engagement reports that after the introduction of the smartphone, the number of people reporting feelings of loneliness jumped 30%.

Loneliness and social isolation are not only taking a toll on people's mental health but also on their physical well-being. The Surgeon General's report states that "Loneliness and social isolation increase the risk for premature death by 26% and 29%, respectively." They have been linked to increases in heart disease and the risk of stroke. The negative health effects of loneliness are the equivalent of smoking 15 cigarettes a day. In addition to physical disease, loneliness and isolation lead to an increase in suicidal thoughts and actions. Citing a 2010 study, the report finds that "Social isolation is arguably the strongest and most reliable predictor of suicidal ideation attempts and lethal suicidal behavior among samples varying in age, nationality, and clinical severity."

We are literally dying from loneliness.

At its heart, however, this is not primarily a mental or physical health crisis. This is a spiritual crisis. It is no surprise that the same Surgeon General's report found a decline in religious engagement and activity:

> Research produced by Gallup, Pew Research Center, and the National Opinion Research Center's General Social Survey demonstrates that since the 1970s, religious preference, affiliation, and participation among U.S. adults have declined. In 2020, only 47% of Americans said they belonged to a church, synagogue, or mosque. This is down from 70% in 1999 and represents a dip below 50% for the first time in the history of the survey question.

As we have cut ourselves off from God, we have also cut ourselves off from each other. The results are devastating. We are not made for isolation; we are made for relationships. This is one of the ways that we bear the image of God. Indeed, the first thing in all creation that God says is not good is for man to be alone.

"Then the Lord God said, 'It is not good that the man should be alone; I will make him a helper fit for him." – Genesis 2:18

Imagine this: Adam is living in direct contact and relationship with God, unhindered by sin, and still, God says it is not good for him to not have someone like himself. People will often say, "All I need is God," but God says this is not true. We need others who are like us to be in relationship with as well. This is not due to any defect in God but reflects how we are created and designed. We are made to be relational beings just as God is a relational being in Himself through the Trinity. The three persons of the Trinity; Father, Son, and Holy Spirit, live in perpetual communion and relationship, each being God, distinct in persons but one in being. Thus, God lives in eternal relationship with one like Himself even though He is One God. This is a deep and profound mystery, but it also forms the core of God's being and existence. We are created in His image, so we, too, are created to not only have relationship with God but with others like us as well. Thus, from Adam, God creates Eve, a helper suitable for him, one who is like him and with whom he can be in relationship.

This is why community has always been at the heart of the Christian faith. In Acts, we read that the early Church met together daily for worship and fellowship. *"And day by day, attending the temple together and breaking bread in their homes, they received their food with glad and generous hearts, praising God and having favor with all the people."* [1] Hebrews warns us against neglecting this fellowship: "*And let us consider how to stir up one another to love and good works, not neglecting to meet together, as is the habit of some, but encouraging one another, and all the more as you see the Day drawing near."* [2]

Given this history and command, it would seem that the Church would be perfectly suited to address this situation. Yet we are prey to this contagion of loneliness as well. During Covid, churches were forced to shut down in-person services for a time. Even after government restrictions were lifted, many churches chose to remain closed, offering services online instead. As a result of this extended disruption of in-person worship, many chose to forgo meeting together even after they were able, and it was perfectly safe to do so. Christianity Today recently reported that 22% of Christians continue to watch services online instead of meeting together in person.

While Covid certainly exacerbated feelings of isolation and loneliness in both the culture and the Church, it did not cause them. The trend, even in the Church, existed before Covid. This points to a deeper problem in the Church that we must address if we are to become the hope to this world we are called to be. That problem is our teaching and conception of the Gospel.

Many things have contributed to our epidemic of loneliness and isolation. One of the main factors is our culture's embrace of hyper-individualism and autonomy. Unlike God's purposes in creation we outlined earlier, hyper-individualism exalts the self above everything. Our only purpose is to actualize our authentic self, however we define that. Anything that allows me to do that is good. Anything I perceive as hindering it is bad. Other people matter only insofar as they help me realize my self-actualization. I owe nothing to them and have no obligation to or for them other than to be my best self. It is this kind of thinking that allows people to believe that the obvious evil of genitally mutilating children so they can live their "true" gender is actually a good thing. It is also what leads these lost children to such desperate beliefs.

In the Church, this has manifested itself by an individualized conception of salvation. The Gospel becomes a highly individualized transaction where I confess my sin, Christ forgives me, and I receive salvation and get to go to heaven when I die. While there is truth in this, it is far from a complete understanding of the whole work of the Gospel. In truth, it is a deeply impoverished view of salvation. That has led many to an impoverished Christian life where they are not receiving or living in the full blessings of what God accomplished in Christ. In a sense, we end up living the same hyper-individualized ethos as the world with a spiritual gloss applied. My quest for self-actualization simply becomes a quest for my self-actualization in Jesus. The focus ultimately remains on the self. God's work of salvation is ultimately for me and my spiritual actualization. A quick perusal of top titles for Christian Living books (*Your Best Life Now, Get Out of Your Head, You Can Change, What if God Wrote Your Bucket List*) reveals a consistent theme: you, you, you. This doesn't represent all Christian books, of course, and I'm not saying there is nothing good in these titles or that their authors are somehow charlatans, but it reveals the subtle influence of the culture on the Church. We must recognize this and intentionally counter it if we are to be all God has called us to be: a community of believers.

The work of the Gospel is far more than just a system for managing sin. It is God's work for the total restoration of His creation. At the heart of creation is relationship, both with God and others. The two greatest commandments are relationship commandments – Love God with all your heart, mind, soul, and strength, and love your neighbor as yourself. The Gospel is ultimately about restoring relationship. The removal of sin is the necessary precondition to that end, but it is not the end in itself.

Many scriptures speak to this, but we will look at Ephesians 2:11-22 where Paul lays this out explicitly.

"Therefore remember that at one time, you Gentiles in the flesh, called "the uncircumcision" by what is called the circumcision, which is made in the flesh by hands— [12] remember that you were at that time separated from Christ, alienated from the commonwealth of Israel and strangers to the covenants of promise, having no hope and without God in the world. [13] But now in Christ Jesus you who once were far off have been brought near by the blood of Christ. For he himself is our peace, who has made us both one and has broken down in his flesh the dividing wall of hostility [15] by abolishing the law of commandments expressed in ordinances, that he might create in himself one new man in place of the two, so making peace, [16] and might reconcile us both to God in one body through the cross, thereby killing the hostility. [17] And he came and preached peace to you who were far off and peace to those who were near. [18] For through him we both have access in one Spirit to the Father. [19] So then you are no longer strangers and aliens, but you are fellow citizens with the saints and members of the household of God, [20] built on the foundation of the apostles and prophets, Christ Jesus himself being the cornerstone, [21] in whom the whole structure, being joined together, grows into a holy temple in the Lord. [22] In him you also are being built together into a dwelling place for God by the Spirit."

In the first two chapters of Ephesians, Paul outlines God's eternal plan of salvation as well as how we receive the gracious gift of God through faith. In this passage, he expands on the purpose of salvation. It is not just about individuals coming to Jesus but about the formation of a community of believers. He uses the example of Jews and Gentiles, who at one time were separated by "a dividing wall of hostility." The Gentiles represent the nations of the world disinherited by God at Babel. After their disinheritance, God called Abraham to form a new nation, one that had never existed but was a creation of God, Israel, to be His vehicle of salvation. They alone carried the instruments of salvation in the Law and Covenants, from which the Gentiles were utterly cut off. Thus, a deep separation existed between the two. Sin had alienated us from God and from each other.

God's plan, however, was always to redeem the nations through Israel and the promised messiah Jesus Christ. Now that Jesus has come, the division between the two has been torn down. No longer are Gentiles cut off from the hope of salvation because in Himself, Jesus has broken down the dividing wall of hostility. Why has He done this? So *"that he might create in himself one new man in place of the two, so making peace, and might reconcile us both to God in one body through the cross, thereby killing the hostility."* Jesus is not just reconciling us to God, He is reconciling us to each other. The Gospel restores us to each other as it restores us to God.

The "one body" referred to in v. 16 may be interpreted as a reference to Jesus, but I believe the stronger reading, both grammatically and theologically, is to see this as the Church as it refers back to the "one new man," which immediately precedes it. In Jesus, we have been made one body, the Church (which is the Body of Christ)[3], and it is as that one Body we are being reconciled to God through the cross. We are being saved together. As Paul says later in the letter, this is the mystery of God revealed: *"that the Gentiles are fellow heirs, members of the same body, and partakers of the promise in Christ Jesus through the gospel."* The Body, the Church, is not an afterthought or a mere organizational principle. It is an essential work of the Gospel meant to restore human relationships rooted in true love for one another as an expression of our faith. It is together that we are "being built into a dwelling place for God by the Spirit." This cannot happen apart from the Church, from our fellow believers.

It is this communal dimension of the Gospel that has been either lost or minimized by our overemphasis on individual salvation. Truly, there is no salvation apart from the Body together. Yes, we must each make a choice for Jesus, but that choice immediately brings us into the Body of Christ, the Church, and it is together as the Church that we are being saved. This is because God's purpose in salvation is the restoration of all the relationships He established at creation. It is only in this way that we can truly be His imagers that reflect His glory. God himself declares this purpose in Revelation 21:3, *"And I heard a loud voice from the throne saying, 'Behold, the dwelling place of God is with man. He will dwell with them, and they will be his people, and God himself will be with them as their God.'"* This is indeed good news to a culture dying of loneliness and isolation. God is working for our restoration, to bring us into life-giving community with Himself and others. It is good news that must be lived and preached if it is to be believed. As Christians, we need to embrace the fullness of the Gospel. More than that, we need to live it. We cannot treat the fellowship as an afterthought or religious duty but as an essential element of living out our faith. Our salvation is not an individualistic affair between us and God but a gracious work to restore us to God's holy community of saints to live and be together. We must resist the culture's temptations to isolation by intentionally choosing to live differently. This means putting down our phones, turning off our screens, and looking beyond ourselves to love and serve others with selfless dedication. Far more than just not neglecting to meet together, we should enthusiastically embrace the fellowship of the Church, recognizing that this may be the most powerful witness to the Gospel that we have today.

Our commitment to community must also go beyond the doors of the church. We should dedicate ourselves to rebuilding the lost social institutions that once served to draw us together. Get involved in your community. Join the PTA, coach a team of kids, visit nursing homes. Even starting a bowling league can be a gospel action. Then, at every turn, be "prepared to make a defense to anyone who asks you for a reason for the hope that is in you." [4]

Acts 2:46-47

[2] Hebrews 10:24-25

[3] See 1 Corinthians 12:27, Ephesians 4:11-13, Colossians 1:24 & 3:15

[4] 1 Peter 3:15

Tommy Briggs is a lead pastor of Gateway Baptist Church and host of The Prayer Closet on 89.3 Yes -Fm. He is a graduate of Bowling Green State University and Winebrenner Theological Seminary (MDiv). Tommy is married to Marianne and has 4 children, ages 18-9.

The 24th Year of This Century

In this the 24th year of this century, let's consider David's powerful and timeless truth spoken in the 24th Psalm. As you read it, let the Holy Spirit speak to you regarding the year 2024.

Psalm 24
A Psalm of David

¹ The earth *is* the LORD's, AND ALL ITS FULLNESS,
The world and those who dwell therein.
² For He has founded it upon the seas,
And established it upon the waters.

³ Who may ascend into the hill of the LORD?
Or who may stand in His holy place?
⁴ He who has clean hands and a pure heart,
Who has not lifted up his soul to an idol,
Nor sworn deceitfully.
⁵ He shall receive blessing from the LORD,
And righteousness from the God of his salvation.
⁶ This *is* Jacob, the generation of those who seek Him,
Who seek Your face. *Selah*

⁷ Lift up your heads, O you gates!
And be lifted up, you everlasting doors!
And the King of glory shall come in.
⁸ Who *is* this King of glory?
The LORD STRONG AND MIGHTY,
The LORD MIGHTY IN BATTLE.
⁹ Lift up your heads, O you gates!
Lift up, you everlasting doors!
And the King of glory shall come in.
¹⁰ Who is this King of glory?
The LORD OF HOSTS,
He *is* the King of glory. *Selah*

It's Gonna Be Worth It

By Daniel J. Angel

For well over two decades, I have had the privilege and the honor to be engaged in the ministry of our Lord Jesus Christ. Like most in the ministry, I started following the normal steps for advancement in the ranks of ministry leadership. I've worked with the kids, youth, and young adults ministries. I became an associate pastor, then a board member, and church treasurer. Without question, my favorite part of ministry has been serving with my beautiful and talented wife, Laura.

For those who may not know, she has a remarkable voice and a God-given gift for leading worship. By default, I have had the privilege of playing guitar on her worship team. Many years ago, she introduced me to one of my favorite songs: Worth It All by Rita Springer. The song is beautiful, but the concept is so encouraging, especially in the midst of the storms of life. A quick synopsis of the song is in order. Basically, the song declares that even when we do not understand God's ways, all of the pain and disappointment we experience while obeying God's call on our lives will be worth it compared to the destination God has for us.

Throughout this journey, I have had front-row seats to watch God move in ways only He can. Likewise, I have had front-row seats to watch and wonder why God did not move in the ways I thought He should. When God is clearly moving, it is so easy to jump on board because it costs us very little. When we are struggling to see God's hand, we need that reminder that even though the road set before us is treacherous, following God's directions is worth it.

Before we get too far into this article, it is essential that I share something with you. Although I sincerely hope this article is beneficial to you, not only am I writing for you: I am writing to me too. There have been so many times that I did not, perhaps still don't, understand God's plans. I'm writing to remind myself of God's faithfulness, mercy, and grace. I'm writing to remind both of us that no matter the circumstances that come on this journey, it's going to be worth it.

The Coward and the Warrior

I'm reminded of Gideon. In Judges 6, we find the story of Gideon, which has become one of my all-time favorite Bible stories. As we see over and over again, the Israelites had once again sinned against God, and He turned them over to the Midianites. The Midianites were so oppressive that Gideon hid in a winepress in the hopes of being able to thresh wheat without his oppressors knowing.

An Angel of the Lord appears to Gideon and says, "*The Lord is with you, mighty warrior.*" The King James Version says, "*mighty man of valor.*" Oh, the irony. Gideon is fearfully hiding to eat scraps, and God sees a mighty warrior. It is amazing how God chooses to see the end product while we get caught up in the process. At this moment, Gideon is a coward. There's no other word to truly describe him. Sure, someone clever could try to argue he was reasonable or strategic. Maybe it was wise or logical to hide from one's enemy. The truth is, Gideon was hiding out of fear. As far as Gideon knew, this could have been his last meal. He gave no thought to war, and there was nothing clever or mighty about his actions.

Of course, we know God had a different perspective. The angel tells Gideon to go and deliver the people of Israel. This mighty warrior replies by stating he is the weakest in his family and his family is the weakest in the community. Again, oh, the irony. Gideon is like an athlete who never plays, but the coach has called his number in crunch time. "Me? But coach, all I do is hand out water during time outs."

It takes a little bit of work, but Gideon is convinced the angel did not make a mistake. However, Gideon still struggles with fear. After the Lord told Gideon to go and destroy the altar of Baal and cut down the Asherah pole, he took ten servants for protection and did it under cover of night. We should give Gideon some credit here. Even though he feared retaliation for destroying the altar, Gideon did as the Lord instructed. You see, Gideon had to make a decision. "Do I stay safe in the winepress or risk it all and follow the Lord onto the battlefield?" Gideon was no longer risking a meager meal but his very life. He had to ask himself if picking up the sword would be worth it. Luckily for Israel, shortly after his encounter with God, we see the mighty warrior Gideon calling men to arms. Gideon decided that following the Lord was going to be worth it.

When the Lord found me, I was hiding in a basement. I had nothing to offer, and like Gideon, I was hoping to make it from one day to the next. I was one step above being homeless and slept from couch to couch. In June of 2000, while lying on an old couch in a basement, I had a dream. Now, I know what you're thinking, "great, he's going to tell me about some random dream he had." I get it; I've been there, but this is not simply a dream. Today, I can see this dream in my mind as if I just woke up. No, this was not simply my subconscious creating random images. This was an encounter with a living God.

I found myself standing on a cubed granite platform. The landscape was full of tornadoes ripping through everything in their path, causing debris to fly in every direction. The sound was truly astounding. I stood frozen in fear. I could not scream, and I could not move. Then a voice spoke in the middle of the chaos. I heard the Voice say, "If you will remain on the rock, the storm will pass by but not destroy you." At that moment, I realized in all of the chaos, I felt no wind from the tornados. I could see them, I could hear them, but I was perfectly safe on that platform. I woke up with tears flowing. I did not begin to cry, I was already weeping while asleep. I rolled off that couch and onto my knees, and I gave my life to the Lord.

So now you're saying, "Cool story, but what does that have to do with me?" I am glad you asked! The landscape before us is full of tornadoes. They come at different stages of our lives. They come in different shapes and sizes. They cause different levels of destruction and chaos. However, one thing is for sure; they will come. As Mathew 5 reminds us, it rains on the just and the unjust. It is in those moments when we need that reminder. It's going to be worth it!

In my dream, the tornadoes were all around. Their appetite for destruction was clearly visible as I looked on in horror. I woke up knowing the Lord was speaking about the future. At first, I was anticipating smooth sailing in rough waters. I thought as long as I stayed on the rock, the storms couldn't hurt me. Of course, that is not what the Lord said in my dream. He said, "The storm will pass by but not destroy you." There was no promise to remove the storm or to lessen its intensity. Rather, the promise was the storm will come, and you will survive.

Story after story, the saints of old were called by God to accomplish unimaginable feats that would place their very lives in harm's way. There was never a promise that God would shield them from pain and heartache. Now, I typically do not gamble, but I would bet every single one of them would agree it was worth it. The Lord found Gideon in a winepress and called him to deliver Israel, but Gideon had to pick up a sword. The Lord found David singing to sheep and called him to be King, but David had to spend years running for his life. The Lord found Joseph beloved by his father and called him to save all of Israel, but he had to endure slavery and imprisonment.

I don't know where the Lord first found you. Likewise, I don't know where the Lord finds you today, but wherever it is, He already knows the end product. He saw the mighty warrior waiting to be called upon, and He sees a mighty warrior today. The Lord may be calling you to full-time ministry or some other specific occupation. Perhaps the Lord wants you to start a business, move your family, or get involved in public policy. Based upon whoever is reading this right now, the possibilities are endless, but one thing is for sure, if God has called you to it, He's calling that warrior within you even if you are hiding in the winepress. Be encouraged. You have been chosen. Pick up your sword. It is going to be worth it.

Things worth having are never easy to obtain

We have all heard the phrase nothing worth having comes easy. If you want a high-paying salary, it takes hard work. If you want rock-hard abs, it takes work. If you want a long-lasting marriage, it takes hard work. If you're like me and you want a long-lasting, LOVING marriage, it takes backbreaking work. (I'm just joking, Laura.) For the most part, we all agree with this concept; things worth having are never easy to obtain.

However, there are times when the work feels like it is simply too hard. Harkening back to Gideon, I am convinced he thought the same thing. In Judges 7, we see Gideon has picked up his sword and is following the calling of the Lord. Gideon raises an army of 32,000 men. Let's put that in perspective for a moment. William the Conqueror took all of England with about 14,000 men, and Gideon doubled William's army. Granted, Gideon is not in command of the largest army in ancient history, but he has gathered a truly formative fighting force.

Then God tells Gideon he has too many men. The Lord tells Gideon to send home every soldier who trembles with fear. Amazingly, 22,000 men went home. I'm shocked every time I read this story, so I know Gideon had to be shocked as well. Now granted, no one wants to go into a fight with support that is so scared they're trembling, but I doubt Gideon thought so many men would be exiting the battlefield.

God does not stop there. The Lord tells Gideon the army is still too big. Gideon has to send home another 9,700 soldiers. Gideon went from the general of an army to the commanding officer of a battalion. I know the Scriptures do not say this, but I can imagine Gideon questioning the new orders from on high. "Wait, what? Lord, I don't understand!"

When God calls you, understanding is not a prerequisite, but obedience is required. God calls us for His glory and not our comfort. The Bible tells us in Isaiah 55 that His ways are not our ways. Gideon only knew what God had called him to do. He did not understand the process God intended to use to free Israel. The Bible is not specific on the logistics, but no one collects a few hundred soldiers, let alone 32,000 men, overnight. That fails to include the weapons and supplies needed to sustain such a fighting force. All of that had to be hard for Gideon. Then there's no doubt in my mind it was also hard for Gideon to send those men home. How could it not? He's called to deliver his nation, and the Lord is sending his forces back to their homes. But here is the beautiful thing; Gideon is doing the hard thing because he recognizes it's worth it. He knows God is the one who has called him to this fight. Even if picking up the sword and going into battle with only 300 men is hard, obeying the call of God is worth it.

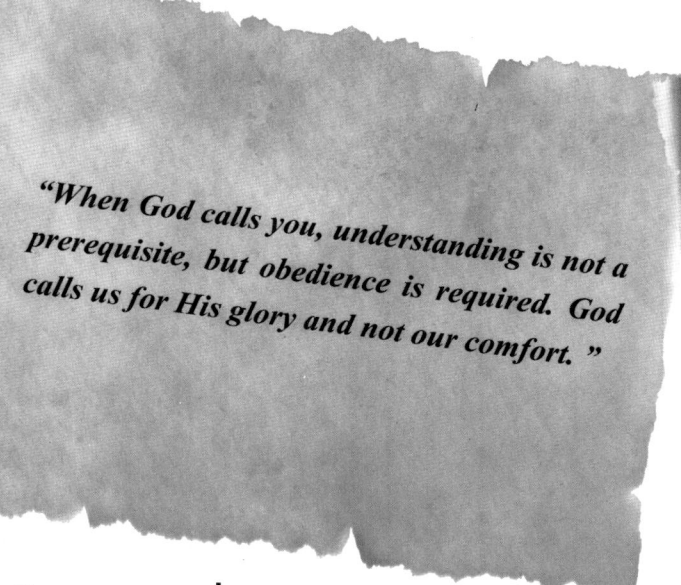

"When God calls you, understanding is not a prerequisite, but obedience is required. God calls us for His glory and not our comfort. "

Be encouraged

Each of us has moments where we do not understand God's plan. We don't understand why He chose us, why He chose this place, and why He chose this time. We all have emerged from a pandemic, and the world appears to be completely upside down. The fundamental truth of biology no longer matters in public education or public policy. The Rights of Parents to raise their children as they see fit are under attack. Buying basic food items, like milk and eggs, are beginning to sell at such a price one would think they were luxury items. Sadly, many in our society have lost their faith and trust in our institutions. Despite the times we are living in, God chose us for this moment!

Pastor, you may not understand why God placed you in a church with members who look more like Saul than Paul. You may not understand why God gave you so many members who know exactly how the ministry should run, but those same visionaries won't sweep the floor or fold a bulletin. You may not understand a lot of things to the point where you want to quit! Don't you dare! If God has called you to that Church, pick up your sword and fight mighty warrior. There are souls to be won, many of them already sitting in that sanctuary! Preach the Gospel with no fear or remorse. When the angel of the Lord appeared to Gideon, Gideon felt like He made a mistake, but Gideon was the right man for the job. Likewise, when God placed you in your position, he did not make a mistake. He called you shortcomings and all. No matter how hard it seems, love the unlovable, feed the hungry, clothe the naked, care for the widow, defend the innocent, and visit the prisoner because it will be worth it.

Mom and Dad, you may not understand why your kids act the way they do or like the things they like. Trust me, when they become teenagers, you will be amazed at the amount of things you do not understand about these so-called bundles of joy. However, from a young age, teach them the truth. Take opportunities to develop a relationship based on trust that continues to grow as they mature. And when they fail, be that parent they know they can run to for restoration. Raising kids is hard. No one has ever done it perfectly right, and I guarantee the grass is always green in someone else's yard. When they rebel, speak the truth in love. Even when they cut you with their tongue, respond in love. God gave those children to you, and He did not make a mistake. The hard work you pour into your child will be worth it.

As we Christians look at our society, we do not understand what is happening. It seems as if we fell asleep one night and woke up in the twilight zone. Guess what! We are not the first generation of believers who have felt this way. Rejoice, for the Lord has chosen us for such a time as this.

In just about every respect, the truth of God's Word is under attack. The battle for the unborn is still ongoing. In fact, since *Dobbs v. Jackson*, the battlefield has expanded from the chambers of the Supreme Court to the legislatures of all fifty states. The battle for the mental health of children is just beginning. While a tiny minority of our society has historically struggled with Satan's lies about their identity, many in society have actively worked to expand those lies to confuse and ensnare every child. The battle for justice in our nation has become perverted. Criminals have become the victims, and victims are now bigots for complaining. Politicians who were once corrupt behind closed doors are now openly using their authority for their own gain of wealth and power. We confuse justice with vengeance. We confuse justice with social justice. If we add a modifier to justice, we no longer have justice. The Midianites have taken the land!

Where are you, Gideon?

I haven't shared my favorite part of Gideon's story. After the Lord tells Gideon to send all but 300 men home, He gives more head-scratching orders. The Lord instructs Gideon to place the most deadly weapons the world had seen to date in their hands. The weapons have struck fear into the hearts of even the most courageous warriors. Gideon was instructed to give his men trumpets, empty jars, and a torch to place in the jars. Wait, what? This whole time, God has told Gideon He would deliver Israel by his hand. The Lord then sends all but a few soldiers home, and the accessories He gives Gideon are not really crafted for war. Then, the beauty of God's plan is put into motion. While Gideon's men blow their trumpets, shatter the jars, and lift up the torches, they shout, "A sword for the Lord and for Gideon." The Midianites turn and run from the fight.

The reason this is my favorite part of the story has nothing to do with the actions of Gideon per se but what those actions demonstrate for us today. Paul tells us in 2 Corinthians 4 that we are jars of clay. In Acts 2, we see the Holy Spirit in the form of fire, and Jehova appeared to Moses in the burning bush. While at war, Gideon's men broke those jars, allowed the fire to be released, and shouted unto God with a voice of victory! When we are willing to be broken ourselves and allow the power of the Holy Spirit to move, what can the Lord use us to accomplish?

We don't need a Church hiding in a winepress. We don't need pastors afraid to lose their tax-exempt status or offend the Pharisees on their boards. We don't need parents wanting to be their child's friend instead of preparing them for their calling. We don't need Christians sacrificing Biblical truth for political convenience. We don't need cowards accepting lies in hopes of avoiding being called a bad name. No, we need Gideons. We need people who want to hide in the winepress but are willing to trust the word of the Lord and pick up their swords. We need those who recognize they may not understand why only 300 hundred soldiers remain, but they will obey orders from their Commander. We need jars of clay willing to allow themselves to be broken so the Lord can be lifted up for all to see.

Beloved, while the battles rage, where are you? Over time, I have found myself in so many different positions. Sometimes, I'm running headlong into the battle. Other times, I need to rest and lick my wounds. I get it, and Gideon gets it too. After Gideon's enemy fled, he had to pursue them and continue to fight. He did not win the war right away. He had no clue how long he would have to fight. However, he knew it was going to be worth it! The Book of Judges tells us that after Gideon fulfilled the call on his life, Israel had forty years of peace.

I have no clue where you are or what you need. There is one thing I know for sure; you would not be reading this if God didn't have a plan for you. I don't know what it is or what it will cost. I do know it will be hard because nothing worth doing is easy. Listen, mighty warrior, get out of the winepress and grab that sword; IT'S GONNA BE WORTH IT!

Daniel J. Angel and his wife, Laura, have served in ministry for 23 years and currently serve at Dayspring AG in Bowling Green, Ohio. The Angels are the proud parents of seven terrific kids. Daniel serves as a member of the Pemberville Village Council and is pursuing a JD from the University of Toledo College of Law.

Select Sayings to the Wise
Proverbs Chapter 24

What follows are some selected sayings from Proverbs 24. The entire book of Proverbs is a collection of sayings to those who would be wise. Listen and apply these Proverbs as you walk through your year ahead serving Jesus:

Do not be envious of evil men, Nor desire to be with them; [2] *For their heart devises violence, And their lips talk of troublemaking.* Proverbs 24:1-2

[3] *Through wisdom a house is built, And by understanding it is established;* [4] *By knowledge the rooms are filled With all precious and pleasant riches.* Proverbs 24:3-4

[5] *A wise man is strong, Yes, a man of knowledge increases strength;* [6] *For by wise counsel you will wage your own war, And in a multitude of counselors there is safety.* Proverbs 24:5-6

If you faint in the day of adversity, Your strength is small. Proverbs 24:10

Deliver those who are drawn toward death, And hold back those stumbling to the slaughter. Proverbs 24:11

[13] *My son, eat honey because it is good, And the honeycomb which is sweet to your taste;* [14] *So shall the knowledge of wisdom be to your soul; If you have found it, there is a prospect, And your hope will not be cut off.* Proverbs 24:13-14

For a righteous man may fall seven times And rise again, But the wicked shall fall by calamity. Proverbs 24:16

[19] *Do not fret because of evildoers, Nor be envious of the wicked;* [20] *For there will be no prospect for the evil man; The lamp of the wicked will be put out.* Proverbs 24:19-20

[24] *He who says to the wicked, "You are righteous," Him the people will curse; Nations will abhor him.* [25] *But those who rebuke the wicked will have delight, And a good blessing will come upon them.* Proverbs 24:24-25

[33] *A little sleep, a little slumber, A little folding of the hands to rest;* [34] *So shall your poverty come like a prowler, And your need like an armed man.* Proverbs 24:33-34

What Does That Mean?

By Jim Pinkelman

The End Times, the rapture, the anti-christ, the tribulation, the beasts, the plagues, the 7 seals, the bowl judgments. These words may bring to mind for you a variety of teaching you may have had over the years. You may even experience a little bit of anxiety or excitement when these topics come up in conversation. Many times in church history, pastors, prophets, apostles, and others have tried to determine what all these words or events mean, how they fit together, and when they will all take place. It is unfortunate that so many have been misled and deceived over the centuries by those who thought they had it all figured out. It seems the result is a Church that shies away from not only talking about the end times but, more generally, prophecy as well. The question is why. Maybe we have just gotten tired of it all, and we have chosen to focus on other parts of the Bible which seem easier to understand. This makes sense because discussions about the love of God and His great forgiveness are easier to grasp than trying to grasp how the entire world will be destroyed and a new Jerusalem will come down from heaven. This is unfortunate because, as 2 Timothy 3:16 says, "**All Scripture** is God-breathed and useful for teaching, for reproof, for correction, for training in righteousness;" (emphasis mine) and let us not exclude verse 17 "so that every man of God may be adequate, equipped **for every good work**." (emphasis mine) So it seems, and rightly so, we need to study all of the Bible to be prepared for every good work.

This thought process comes up in a senior Bible class I teach at a local Christian school. Part of the class is a journey into the book of Revelation. In our discussions, I regularly state that I never want to definitely say that the events in Revelation are happening on such and such a date and such and such a place. However, we do talk about how we know when the season is upon us because Jesus makes some things pretty clear in the Olivet Discourse. As I prepared for the study, it became clear to me rather quickly that there were other passages which we needed to understand before we got to Revelation. For example, there are passages in Daniel, Matthew, and Thessalonians that need to be understood and examined to give context to Revelation. This was beginning to look like a bigger endeavor than I had planned for the class. So we got started, and soon, I had one student ask, "If we can't know for sure what Revelation is all about, then why bother?"

I was ready for that question and answered with 2 Timothy 3:16. That did not satisfy the student at all. I continued by explaining verse 17. I added, "There is a time coming when these events will take place, and the world will want to know what is happening. Who is the world going to turn to for answers? Christians! We need to know so we can be the light in their darkness. Essentially, being equipped for every good work and leading people out of darkness seems like good work." That seemed to satisfy the students' questions.

Why do I share this story from my senior Bible class? It's because I believe there are many of us who say, "Why bother?" as well. However, I also believe there is something in all of us that wants to know about the end times. Additionally, I believe that there is something in our spirit which yearns for Christ's return. We grow weary living out our lives here on earth. This is our journey. Even though we have this yearning inside of us, we ignore it for the most part because our lives are too busy to give the topic any attention. However, we must give it our attention; it is part of His Word to us, so there **is** something useful in its study.

I have come to the conclusion that we just have not been given the tools to help us understand His Word. Don't get me wrong, the good Lord has provided wonderful teachers for us to learn from, but ultimately we need to take the responsibility ourselves to study the Word. An athlete cannot just watch or listen to good athletic training videos and seminars to become great. There comes a time when the athlete needs to get up and practice for himself or herself if he or she wants to be any good at his or her sport. To that end, I would like to give you some tools to help you not only study the passages connected to the end times but will also ultimately help you study the entire Bible.

Let's keep a few things in mind as we start.

1. We will never completely know the mind of God while here on earth. There are many gaps in our understanding which will be discussed later.

2. If the interpretation of the passage you are studying makes sense (based on study) then it is probably the right sense.

3. Since scriptures are God-breathed (by the Holy Spirit), then seek the Holy Spirit in your interpretation. However, be careful not to:
   a. Over spiritualize
   b. Over allegoricalize
   c. Over symbolize

4. There are so many other resources to draw from to help in your study.
   a. Bible Gateway or other Bible database
   b. Blue Letter Bible
   c. Interpreting the Scriptures (by Conner and Malmin)

So, what are these gaps in our understanding referred to in point number one above? We have to understand that in our modern culture, many things have been lost, and here are some of those.

1. **The Linguistic Gap**. Language changes so much. Even in our modern culture, a word may mean something different today than it did a year ago. Imagine that happening over a thousand years or even across cultures. I am continually hearing new words the students use, and I have to ask them what it means, not because I am old, it is just a new word.

2. **The Cultural Gap.** No one today has lived in Bible times, and we don't have a time machine to take us back to understand the way culture operated. Think about how women's roles in society have changed since the 1950s. We have archaeology to help us uncover many artifacts about Biblical culture and help confirm things in the Bible, yet these are still artifacts. There is no owner's manual to help us know how things were used.

3. **The Geographical Gap**. The landscape doesn't change that quickly, but our understanding of the land and climates is very much lacking. For example, let's look at Mt. Siani. Do you know how tall it is? How long did it take Moses to climb it? How about the Red Sea? Do you have an understanding of how big that is? The list is endless of these types of things we don't understand.

4. **The Historical Gap.** Kings, queens, governments, politics, who conquered whom, who lived, when and how did they come into power is the beginning of a long list of history we don't understand. Again, archaeology helps us date these things but by no means gives us a complete picture of what went on. An example I use in class is, why did Jesus have to see so many people before Pilate released him to be crucified? He first went before the Jewish leaders, then Pilate, then Herod, and then back to Pilate. An understanding of who was in charge and the limits of their authority makes this clearer.

I don't present these gaps to discourage you from actually taking up the study of scriptures. It is my hope that understanding where we fall short will take some of the pressure off us to get it right. We won't always get it right, but it is a noble pursuit because, as stated before, all Scripture is God-breathed and useful. So I say, why not make the noble effort and learn something along the way? Here are a few principles of interpretation that may help you on the way. These are all from a book I use in my class. (*Interpreting the Scriptures*) There are many more principles in the book other than what I will discuss here, and I encourage you to get the book and learn the others for yourself.

1. **The Context principle.** This is the idea that we should not take scripture out of its context. An extreme example would be "Jesus wept," and then conclude that Jesus cried all the time. Obviously, this is not true. The idea is that a passage needs to agree with the theme of the section it is in, as well as the book it is in. Further, the interpretation should agree with the themes of the testament and with the themes of the Bible. If there is a contradiction with any of these themes, then the interpretation is wrong. This is pretty simple but can be misused.

2. **The Comparative Mention principle.** Considering themes of the Bible, we can also find places where there are similar words or, phrases, or concepts used in various parts of the Bible. How Jesus fulfilled the Old Testament prophecy is a good study to undertake. There are over 350 passages, including many direct quotes, in the Old Testament that are fulfilled in the New Testament. In my Master's thesis, I compared and contrasted Exodus with Revelation. This seems incredible, but there are many connections to the two books. Other topics which can be compared are principles, events, symbols, persons, places, and parables.

3. **The Symbolic principle**. Many times in the Bible, things are just what they are; however, there are symbolic themes that run through the Bible. Water and wind are a couple of these things, which many times are symbolic of something else. Creatures are symbolic: Jesus is a lion, for example. Plants, actions, names, direction, colors, and numbers (which a whole study can be done here) are many of the things which have symbolic meaning.

4. **The Typical principle**. This can be a bit of a challenge to understand and does require the use of other principles. The best example is the idea that Moses is a type of Jesus. In other words, as you look over the entirety of Moses' life in many ways, there are parallels to Jesus' life. This makes sense because the entirety of the Old Testament really points to the Messiah of the New Testament.

5. **The Allegorical principle**. An allegory is a bit different than a metaphor or a simile. For that matter, an allegory is really an extended metaphor. We can say that Jesus is the rock as a metaphor, but we can see so many times when the rock is used in the entirety of the scriptures. He is the rock of my salvation, He is the cornerstone, He is a firm foundation, are just a few examples. The stories of Narnia are allegories where Aslan represents Jesus.

6. **The Numerical and Color principle**. While these seem self-explanatory on the surface, and they are, add to them the number of times certain numbers and colors show up across the whole Bible. You begin to see a thread that weaves scripture together and makes it a whole picture. Take the number 40: 40 days of the flood, 40 years in the desert, 40 days Moses, Elijah, and Jesus fasted, Ezekiel laying on his right side for 40 days.

In the book *Interpreting the Scriptures,* there are 24 different principles of interpretation. That is a lot, and I will certainly not cover all of them here. We must be careful not to take each one separately without using the others. While not all the principles will apply to each passage, several of them will. I believe as you begin your study of a passage, a beautiful picture of God's purpose for man will begin to be painted for you. Will it ever be finished? I don't believe so. Just like putting a puzzle together, the whole picture becomes clearer and clearer as time goes by.

In the beginning, I mentioned Revelation, and I would like to take just one passage and show you how each of these principles works through that passage. Let's look at Revelation chapter 4 and see how we can use these principles to help us understand the chapter.

¹ After this I looked, and there before me was a door standing open in heaven. And the voice I had first heard speaking to me like a trumpet said, "Come up here, and I will show you what must take place after this." 2 At once I was in the Spirit, and there before me was a throne in heaven with someone sitting on it. 3 And the one who sat there had the appearance of jasper and ruby. A rainbow that shone like an emerald encircled the throne. 4 Surrounding the throne were twenty-four other thrones, and seated on them were twenty-four elders. They were dressed in white and had crowns of gold on their heads. 5 From the throne came flashes of lightning, rumblings and peals of thunder. In front of the throne, seven lamps were blazing. These are the seven spirits of God. 6 Also in front of the throne there was what looked like a sea of glass, clear as crystal.

In the center, around the throne, were four living creatures, and they were covered with eyes, in front and in back. 7 The first living creature was like a lion, the second was like an ox, the third had a face like a man, the fourth was like a flying eagle. 8 Each of the four living creatures had six wings and was covered with eyes all around, even under its wings. Day and night they never stop saying: " 'Holy, holy, holy is the Lord God Almighty, who was, and is, and is to come."
⁹ Whenever the living creatures give glory, honor and thanks to him who sits on the throne and who lives for ever and ever, ¹⁰ the twenty-four elders fall down before him who sits on the throne and worship him who lives for ever and ever. They lay their crowns before the throne and say: ¹¹ "You are worthy, our Lord and God, to receive glory and honor and power, for you created all things, and by your will they were created and have their being."

The Context Principle.

Let's first consider the major themes of Revelation itself. First, we know it is a book of prophecy. Prophecy can and does make predictions concerning the future and also makes proclamations about God and His character. This will be important to know when we discuss the allegorical principle. Additionally, Revelation can be seen to be about God's sovereignty, Christ's return, judgment, and hope in eternity. The question we ask ourselves then is, "Does this passage fit into the themes of Revelation?" The answer is, "Yes!" This will become more evident as we use the other principles to reveal these themes. For example, one of the creatures looks like an eagle. Symbolically, an eagle represents God's sovereignty. It is also understood that the major theme of the entire Bible is God's plan to redeem His people to himself. Chapter 4 sets the stage for this plan to unfold for His creation. None of these themes contradict our understanding of chapter 4 so we must be on the right track.

The Comparative principle.

There are many things we can compare in this passage. Here are two that we will explore: In verse 1, we find the word trumpet, and typically, we conclude that this is the voice of God. However, let's just confirm this with a few other passages in scripture. Isaiah 27:13 is a word of prophecy and seems to indicate that the Lord will call all those to Him to worship on the holy mountain. Matthew 24:31 says His angels will be sent out with a trumpet call in the last days. 1 Thessalonians 4:16 describes the trumpet call of God as well. Additionally, Revelation 1:10 and 11:12 also describe the voice of God as a trumpet. Simply it seems we can conclude a trumpet is something making a call to believers, and more specifically, it is God's voice calling to His people. In verse 5, we find lightning, rumblings, and peals of thunder. If taken literally, we might conclude that it is about to rain in heaven and pretty seriously, too. However, if we look for other passages in the Bible, we may be able to understand better what these mean. One of the first times we see these words in scripture is in Exodus 19:16, when God's glory descends on Mount Sinai. This is repeated again in Exodus 20:18. Psalms describes this as well in 77:18 and 97:4, both describing His presence. Daniel describes a man with a face like lightning in 10:6, and in Matthew, Jesus describes His own return as lightning. Additionally, Revelation also has other references to lightning and all in reference to God's presence; Revelation 8:5, 11:19, and 16:18. It seems, at the very least, lighting, rumblings, and peals of thunder refer to God's presence in chapter 4. It can also be understood that neither of these understandings contradicts any of the major themes of Revelation or the Bible as a whole. So, we may be correct in our understanding of these things. So far, so good.

The Symbolic Principle.

Let's examine the creatures described in the second half of verse 6 and verse 7. The first thing we need to understand is that John saw these creatures, and they are real, but they also have symbolic meaning in the heavenlies.There are other beliefs that suggest that John had a dream, and what he saw was just that, and nothing about it was real. While that seems reasonable, we will accept here that John saw real creatures that have symbolic meaning. He saw a lion, an ox, a man, and an eagle. Each had eyes all over them and had six wings. Let's just focus on the types of creatures here. Just as a comparison (Comparative Principle), these same creatures are described in Ezekiel 1:5-10. These creatures symbolically represent God's character. The lion represents God's power; a lion is very powerful, the king of the animals. An ox shows God's faithfulness. In the Old Testament, an ox was there to work the fields and be faithful to its owner for its entire life. The man symbolizes God's intelligence. Man is the only intelligent, creative being in all of creation. The eagle reveals God's sovereignty. Even in our own culture, we see the eagle as majestic as it sores in the sky. Interestingly, the gospels also reveal these same creatures as themes in their writing. Matthew shows Christ as a Lion of Judah, Mark shows Christ as a servant, Luke, Christ as the perfect human, and John as the Son

of God, exalted and divine. Notice here we showed how these creatures are symbolic of God's character. We also compared them with other scriptures and themes to get a better, clearer understanding of their meaning. Hopefully, you see that while each of these principles can stand alone, they will be used together.

The Typical Principle.

This principle may not just deal with one word or verse, though it could. More likely, it deals with concepts such as persons, offices, institutions, or events. In Revelation chapter 4, we get a good look at the throne room in heaven. Later, we find this room is also in Revelation in the New Jerusalem. So, a type (in this example, the throne room) is a prophetic representation of one thing prefiguring another. Where do we find a detailed description of the temple and all its details? It can be found in Exodus 25-40. God gives a very detailed description of the tent of meeting all the utensils and clothing and rituals for Israel to follow. This is a prophetic representation of the throne room in heaven, which we find in Revelation chapter 4. For a more in-depth study, we could explore how Christ is also a type of temple and how we, as believers filled with the Holy Spirit, are also types of the temple, all reflecting His glory here on earth. This is a fascinating study, which would be a paper in and of itself. It seems appropriate then to understand why, after addressing the churches, John begins with a description of the throne room in heaven. The temple has been reflected throughout all human history in one way or another and is the focus of all worship, which we see the 24 elders engaging in, and they are our example.

The Allegorical Principle.

Before we begin this principle, we have to decide if the passage under study is truly allegorical in nature. If it is not, then we cannot use this principle for the passage we are studying. Since we have already concluded that Revelation chapter 4 is prophetic and is something that John actually saw, then more than likely, it is not an allegorical passage. The passage has been interpreted as such by some, but the conclusions drawn don't fit with the entirety of Scripture. There are many examples of an allegory, and one such example is John 15:1-10. This passage talks about the vine and the branches. It is an allegory because there are several things that refer to other things, for example, the vine and the branches and marriage. By studying vineyards and marriage, we get a better understanding of our relationship with Christ. It is not possible to find these types of comparisons in Chapter 4 of Revelation based on some of our previous conclusions. This example shows that even though several principles may be used together to understand a passage, by no means will all of them be used.

The Color/Number Principle.
Following are a list of colors and numbers found in Chapter 4 and their meaning:

Rainbow
Reminder of God's promise to Noah and, more generally, His promises to us

24 Thrones
12 tribes of Israel, 12 Apostles - divine government apostolic fullness

12 x 12 =144
Ultimate creation (this may be a stretch)

White
Purity, clean - symbolizing righteousness

Gold
God's love and protection, blessing, favored

4
Number of earth, creation, world. (Directions, seasons, elements: wind, water, earth, fire) (Medieval times: yellow bile, black bile, blood, phlegm) Also winds of judgment Jeremiah 49:35-39

Hopefully, these few examples help you to understand the depth at which you can understand scriptures. It is not an easy task, but it can be incredibly rewarding. Consider a couple of verses, one from Jesus and one from Paul. In Matthew 24: 23-25, Jesus warns us there will be false christs and prophets, and they will perform signs and miracles. In Acts 20:29-31, Paul also warns there will be savage wolves that will come from among them, and we should be on guard against them. Today it seems there is a rise of false teachings rising up even in the Church. What better way to prepare ourselves than to be able to study the Scriptures for ourselves and not rely on others' interpretations of the Word. Please understand not everyone is a false christ, prophet, or teacher. However, we need to be aware, just as Jesus and Paul warn us. I am grateful I sit under a man who takes the Word of God seriously and presents the Truth to the congregation. There are times I do go home and "fact check" what was said with the tools I presented here in this paper, and I encourage you to do the same. Let me leave you with this scripture: Proverbs 27:17 tells us, "As iron sharpens iron, so one man sharpens another." Wise words when it comes to the study of Scripture.

"What better way to prepare ourselves than to be able to study the Scriptures for ourselves and not rely on others' interpretations of the Word."

Credits
Interpreting the Scriptures, Kevin J. Conner and Ken Malmin, ISBN 0-914936-20-4
All scriptures are taken out of the *New International Version.*

Jim Pinkelman, a lifelong northwest Ohio native, currently lives in Haskins with his wife, Suzie. After many years in the woodworking industry, God called him to use his gifts to build up people instead of building things. He now coaches and directs theatre for high school students.

Moms and Daughters, Aunts and Angels

By Robin Sullivan

"Are your bags packed?" she asked with that ever so convicting look in her eyes, piercing straight to the bottom of my heart. Man! There were times when my mother's remarks to me either angered me or made me want to vomit. Sorry, but that's the raw truth.

When she would pull out the "bags packed" line, I would joke to myself that she just wanted me to "get out of Dodge." I'm pretty sure I was right about that sometimes, but my mom's intention mainly was to cause me to think over my ongoing poor choices in life and what the consequences of those choices might be. She was reminding me that there would be a day when I would need to give an account of my life to my Maker. Was I ready for that?

"Who is?" I thought.

Mom was doing her downright best to jostle me towards the cross, but *The preaching of the cross is foolishness to those who are perishing, but to us who are being saved, it is the power of God."*   1 Corinthians 1: 18

With a mountain of sin under my belt, I finally came to know the Lord and His great salvation. What I once considered "foolishness" had now become the truth that set me free. Romans 2:4 tells us, "It is His kindness that leads us to repentance." Let me tell you, it sure helps to have a momma who is pleading in the courts of heaven on your behalf.

"The prayers of the saints rise up before God and then God acts on earth."
Revelation 8:3

It was the bicentennial year, and I was living on the Jersey shore with a friend and her boyfriend, working as a barmaid at this restaurant called Pier One. The fishermen all came in for lunch, starving and ever so thirsty, as they had been out since 5:00 or 6:00 am to haul in their catch. All I know is I made more money that summer than I ever had in my life. I really lived it up, too, I gotta tell you!

I had been dating this guy named Tom, who was living in Maryland (we went to college in DC). He would hitchhike to see me most weekends. There was this one time he could not come, and he had suggested that at some point, it would be nice if I made the effort to go and see him. Well, I didn't have a car; I was fortunate that I could walk to work. So I did what any normal girl would do in the 70s, I hitchhiked all the way from Toms River to Hyattsville, MD, which was just outside of the northeastern quadrant of DC.

I know… crazy!

I know… dangerous!

But I opted to see this as an adventure.

The first ride was a station wagon (for those who are unfamiliar, that's a stretched-out SUV), hauling a group of construction guys who kindly got me high.

The second was what we referred to as a boat, an older Lincoln that had a full bar in the backseat, and the guy who was driving was traveling with his "niece." He said he'd be glad to take me close to Baltimore as long as I made them drinks. No problem. I was a professional, after all.

The third was an 18-wheeler, known to be one of the more reliable rides, as they would help you find your next ride more often than not. Mind you, I had never EVER hitchhiked by myself; I had only been accompanied by a guy.

I was relieved to be close to my destination, thinking to myself how much fun it was going to be to surprise Tom.

The trucker was a CB operator, but he turned it off so that our conversation would not be interrupted.

One thing that stood out about this ride was how interested this middle-aged man was in my personal life. He asked me about my family. What were my parents like? How many siblings did I have? What was I studying in college? Where did I work? And on and on. I thought he was just a nice guy, like most truckers that I had met. But then, this seemingly kind man took a sudden turn off the highway, and I instantly knew he had dark intentions and the sun had already set.

Jesus said, *"The devil comes only to steal, kill and destroy, but I have come that you might have life and that more abundantly."* John 10:10

The effects of the drugs and alcohol suddenly lifted, and I developed a plan, rehearsing it over and over in my mind.

I would wait until he came to a dead stop, pull the lock-up, grab my knapsack, fling open the door, jump down, and run like a bandit toward the highway. Again, I rehearsed it: dead stop, unlock, grab, fling, jump, run, run, run.

See, this was not a truck stop that had a restaurant; it was a place where truckers go only to sleep, with a sole cinderblock bathroom and one dusty light. He stopped, and I began executing my escape. He reached back to open a curtain behind us, revealing a bed, as he lunged toward me, my exit plan already in full swing.

He chased me, yelling obscenities, and as I passed that solitary cinderblock bathroom, I smashed right into two tall, very handsome young men who said, "Whoa, whoa, where are you going, young lady?"

I explained, "That man…" turning behind me and incredibly relieved to see him running as fast as he could back to his 18-wheeler, "He, he was about to…"

One said, "Well, he's long gone now, and you are safe. Where are you headed?" It was at that point that I noticed there were two sleek sports cars, one was bright yellow and the other bright blue, parked right there in front of me.

Obviously, there was no one else around, so I asked them, "Where did you guys come from?" I remember them looking at each other, smiling, and simultaneously saying, "Europe."

Oh, of course, that makes perfect sense. Europe?

One of them, the blonde, motioned to the cars and interjected, "Yeah, we just got these shipped over."

My face scrunched in question. What did that mean?

The other asked if I preferred country music or rock 'n' roll. I responded with rock 'n' roll, to which he said, "Ok, come with me. We'll take you to Hyattsville."

I was silent the whole ride, noting that they drove in tandem, and I thought that was cool. When we arrived in town, we stopped at a Burger King, and I went to the pay phone to call Tom. "Surprise! Pick me up, ok? Wait until I tell you what happened!"

I returned to the table where the guys had been sitting, but they had vanished. I ran outside and didn't even see the taillights of the hotrods. Bummer! I didn't even get to thank them for rescuing me. Thinking their departure was odd, I shrugged my shoulders and concluded that they weren't interested in meeting my boyfriend. I was,

however, grateful that they just "happened" to be there to rescue me from needing to run down the highway and save me from my frightening situation.

Tom borrowed a car and drove me home a couple of days later. Upon arriving at work the following day, there was a message that my mom had called, and they said she was adamant that I call back.

Me: "Ma?"

Mom: "What was going on at 9 p.m. Friday night?"

Me: "Oh, nothin'…"

Mom: "The Holy Spirit drew me to my knees for you. It was very intense, don't lie to me. What was going on?"

Me: "Nothing, Mom!"

Mom: "One day, I will know."

"For there is nothing hidden that will not be disclosed, and nothing concealed that will not be known or brought out into the open." Luke 8:17

I know the Word of God says, "*And you shall know the truth and the truth shall set you free*". To me, however, the truth was repulsive. I didn't want to hear it. Truth be told, I liked my sin, and I was so deep in it that I knew beyond a shadow of a doubt that there was no way any prayer was going to save me from the consequences of the things that I had done. Religion taught me that. Nice, huh?

Salvation is a miracle.

How did the Spirit ever penetrate my obscenely warped way of thinking? A miracle.

How did God rescue me from disaster? A miracle.

Now that I know THE Truth, it saddens me to think that there are so many people who think that they can somehow compensate for their own sins or justify what they have

"…it saddens me to think that there are so many people who think that they can somehow compensate for their own sins or justify what they have done as so minor…"

done as so minor with the token, "I never killed anybody, and I never robbed a bank." Well, at least I was smart enough to know that my wrongs were so atrocious there was no way out. So that deceptive phrase "Eat, drink, and be merry!" suited me just fine. I was a degenerate.

One thing I knew for sure was there weren't enough Our Fathers and Hail Marys for me to recite that could cover my sin, and that's the truth. That *is* the truth.

How feeble would that be? Now I know that what it takes to be forgiven is a contrite heart; the wall of pride must be demolished, and a sacrifice for my sin must be made.

I may not have been ready, but God always is. For my sins to be covered, blood had to be shed, and not just any blood. It took the ultimate sacrifice of the Father Himself to send His one and only Son to die for my sins. It was an act so profound it makes me quiver on the inside to think of this great salvation.

"In fact, according to the law of Moses, nearly everything was purified with blood. For without the shedding of blood, there is no forgiveness." Hebrews 9:22

Grateful beyond measure is what I am, that the great I AM would love me so much. Praise His Name forever! As King David put it, *"May those who love your salvation repeatedly shout, "God is great!"* Psalms 70:4

Recently, I had a conversation with the only one left of the Mohicans in my family, my Aunt Mary. She is teetering at age 95, and her old body is not behaving as it did even as recently as two years ago when she was still walking a minimum of two miles a day. Her mind, however, is as "sharp as a tack."

The painful truth is that she, like a much younger me, has not yet "packed her bags."

I mentioned the phrase with the hopes that we could talk about spiritual things, and she emphatically said, "I always hated it when your mother would say that!" I confessed to her how much I hated it, too! Marybelle raised her blond eyebrows at that response. Then, with a huge smile, I continued, "But it didn't bother me at all once I knew for certain that my bags were packed." At that moment, one could cut the air with a knife.

Lend me your ear.

Due to the fact that her physical not-so-well body isn't properly functioning, she is no longer able to live at home. Believe me, she was mad as the proverbial wet hen about that. Marybelle (her nickname) was a teacher in the local school system for many years; she was stylish, savvy, and single. She has a penchant for pink to the extent that her front and side doors were painted Pepto Bismal pink. An avid reader (and to this day), she traveled, took dance exercise classes, and made homemade chocolate fudge for ice cream. She took me to the beach whenever I begged. She loved going to the mall just before it closed for some unknown reason, but at least it was a trip to the mall! She provided a lovely, comfortable home for her parents, and when Pop Sullivan passed away, she doted on her mother, with whom she also fought. They loved each other vehemently but clashed as mothers and daughters often do. Why is that?!

In any case, one of the commandments plainly states, *"Honor your father and your mother."* Let's not mess with that!

I visited Marybelle recently in her new habitat, which she hates, which breaks my heart. I was honored to assist her and even take her outside to enjoy a warm breeze and play some gin rummy. She handed me a notebook and asked if I would put the phone numbers of my siblings and my cousins in a nice, neat fashion. I did.

I gently told her there was one more I'd like to add, only there is no phone number.

She looked up.

Smiling softly, I said, "Jesus. If you call on Him, He will answer."

A very long pause followed.

She quietly told me the priest came by and asked if she wanted to receive communion and did she also want to go to confession.

I said, "How did that go?"

Marybelle responded, "I told him that I had not neglected going to mass, on TV, of course. But yes, I would like to participate in both." Then she added, "Too bad I didn't die then because he absolved me of all my sin."

To which I said, "You can *always* confess to God, and you can *always* have communion with Him in your heart. You can *always* call Him, and you never get voice mail with Him."

"He shall call upon Me, and I will answer him: I will be with him in trouble; I will deliver him and honor him." Psalm 91:15

The only thing that I can do now is pray and then some. No one can make the decision to let the wall of pride down except the individual whose wall it is. It's excruciating when you realize that someone whom you love so much feels like they are ok, and you know they are not. Nothing aptly describes this. I just truly believe that one day, Marybelle will go to that notebook, find my name, and tell me, "I'm calling you to tell you that I called Him, and He answered me."

I cannot wait to see her pink Samsonite.

Robin was rescued from darkness on a Friday night in November of 1978 and is more in awe of the Lord now than ever. She is positively blown away that He chose her to be a DJ for Him, allowing her the opportunity to proclaim the Gospel Story on Christian radio for over 40 years. She is currently heard on Proclaim FM 102.3. Visit robinsullivan.com.

Notable Events in the 24th Year of Past Centuries

1024 BC

The year it is believed that David faced and killed the giant Goliath in Israel.

1224

After receiving a vision while praying on Mount Verna, Francis of Assisi receives a stigmata, or wounds resembling the wounds of Christ's crucified body.

1524

A Florentine Navigator named Giovanni Verrazano was the first to discover what became New York Bay.

1724

Glassblower Daniel Gabriel Fahrenheit presents a paper to the Royal Society of Lond proposing a system to make thermometers.

1824

John Quincy Adams became President of the United States even though Andrew Jackson had received more of the popular vote. Without enough electoral votes, however, the contest was decided in the House of Representatives. General Lafayette made his first return to the United States since the completion of the Revolutionary War.

1924

Ellis Island is closed as an immigration entry point into the US after being in service for 32 years.
Two US Army planes complete the first round-the-world flight in 175 days, covering 26,000 miles.
The first Winter Olympics were completed in Chamonix, France. 16 nations participated, with Norway winning the most medals, garnering a total of 17.

Discipling Others

By Jeremy Smallman

Most of us know "The Great Commission" given to us by Jesus just before He ascends to heaven in Matthew 28:18-20:

"And Jesus came up and spoke to them, saying, "All authority has been given to Me in heaven and on earth. Go therefore and make disciples of all the nations, baptizing them in the name of the Father and the Son and the Holy Spirit, teaching them to observe all that I commanded you; and lo, I am with you always, even to the end of the age."

He tells us to go and "make disciples." But what does that mean? When you decide to do it, what is it? How is it done? What does it look like? These are the questions I will be answering here.

But first, I will begin with the end because I am inviting you to do this *now*.

Who: You!
What: Build close, personal relationships with a few people.
How: Meeting one-on-one with them regularly.
Why: For true, lasting change in that person and to show them the way of Jesus.
When: Now!

What is "make disciples"?

This can be interpreted as "make relationships." At its core, it develops a bond and connection with another person. It is openness and trust between both people and genuine care for the individual you are discipling. Of course, it is also teaching, training, and leading them in the Word of God and the ways of Jesus. By imitating Jesus and emulating His character, you are showing that person Jesus and how to be a disciple of Him. Conversations around the things of God and teaching the Word of God will come naturally as the relationship progresses. This is a long-term relationship that takes commitment. Since our Heavenly Father created us for relationships, this kind of commitment should come easily and naturally.

To make my point further, I am going to pull out two quotes from the expanded definition of the Greek word behind "make disciples" from The Hebrew-Greek Keyword Study Bible because it states it so beautifully and accurately:

"The word suggests (in a religious context) the deep shaping of character and the cultivation of a worldview through a close, personal relationship between the [disciple] and the [teacher]."

"The goal of discipleship is not simply the attaining of information, but the experience and enjoyment of fellowship."

So, remember, the relationship comes first. It's not all about teaching the Word of God, correcting doctrine, and right or wrong beliefs, though that's part of it. Have genuine care and love for the person you are discipling, and all that other stuff will follow.

The purpose and the result

The goal is to bring that person into a relationship with Jesus, making them a disciple of Jesus. We are to teach them to be imitators of Jesus, not of us. We want them to become followers of Jesus, not followers of us. Then they will, in turn, make other disciples. Disciples make disciples, and it will have an exponential growth effect when it continues. This is not "I hope that person disciples others" or "that person *should* disciple others now." When you have truly discipled a person, they *will* disciple others! It's the natural side-effect of the impact of having been discipled.

One important benefit of spending personal time with Jesus is that it is a time of *rest* and *refreshment*. We pour much of ourselves into those around us, in addition to the daily demands of life, so we need to "fill our tank" to stay focused and energized to continue serving Him and others. Jesus *wants* us to take breaks and get some rest. We see this in Mark 6:30-32. Jesus had just sent out His twelve disciples to preach and minister to the people of Israel. Upon returning, there were still "*many people coming and going, and they did not even have time to eat,*" and Jesus says to His disciples:

"Come away by yourselves to a secluded place and rest a while."

Jesus found time to rest Himself, and He encourages us to do the same.

Next, Jesus prepares for choosing His disciples. In Luke 6:12, Jesus spends all night praying to God before choosing the ones that He would develop a closer relationship with and disciple. The Word does not say what Jesus was praying specifically, but based on the timing of this, it's logical to think Jesus was seeking God for wisdom and direction for whom He should choose as His closest disciples. It's even possible that God gave him the number of disciples to choose - twelve. What we learn from this is before you go and look for a few people to disciple, pray that God reveals to you whom (and how many) you should choose to disciple or that He would bring the right people into your life for you to disciple. Let this be Holy Spirit-led.

After that, Jesus actively sought out the ones He was to disciple. The most familiar example of this starts in Matthew 4:18 when Jesus calls Peter, Andrew, James, and John to follow Him and be His disciples. Jesus sought them out. He didn't wait to be asked. Don't sit back and wait for someone to come into your life or for something just to happen. Be intentional in seeking someone to disciple, and keep looking until you've found a match. I suggest the same if you are looking for someone to disciple you. Don't give up.

From there, Jesus spent a good portion of His time with His disciples alone. We see evidence of this in a seemingly passing comment in John 18:2, speaking about Jesus going to the Garden of Gethsemane on the night of His betrayal:

"Now Judas also, who was betraying Him, knew the place, for Jesus had often met there with His disciples."

Jesus went to that garden often, alone with His disciples, just as He did here the last night before His death. Jesus also spent a lot of time with His disciples explaining and expounding upon His teachings. For example, in Matthew 13:10-23, Jesus tells His disciples, *"To you it has been granted to know the mysteries of the kingdom of heaven..."* and goes on to explain the parable of the sower. Only with His disciples did He reveal such things. From all this, we learn that one-on-one time with those you are discipling is important and needs to be a priority.

Jesus chose twelve men to be His followers, but even among those twelve, He chose only three to develop a close, intimate bond with: Peter, James, and John. It was only those three that Jesus took high on a mountain to see Him transfigured and to see Moses and Elijah (Matthew 17). It was only those three Jesus took deeper into the garden on the night He was betrayed and allowed them to see Him in great distress (Mark 14:32-34). Jesus limited the number of close followers He had and further limited intimate access to Himself for a deeper relationship. This tells me that we also need to limit the number of people we disciple at one time to be effective. God knows what your capacity is, and the Holy Spirit will guide you to ensure you are not stretching yourself too thin. Be sure to listen and be obedient as you seek out those who may be open to your discipling them so you keep a healthy balance.

We need to see one more characteristic of Jesus because it is foundational to discipling others: He loved His disciples.

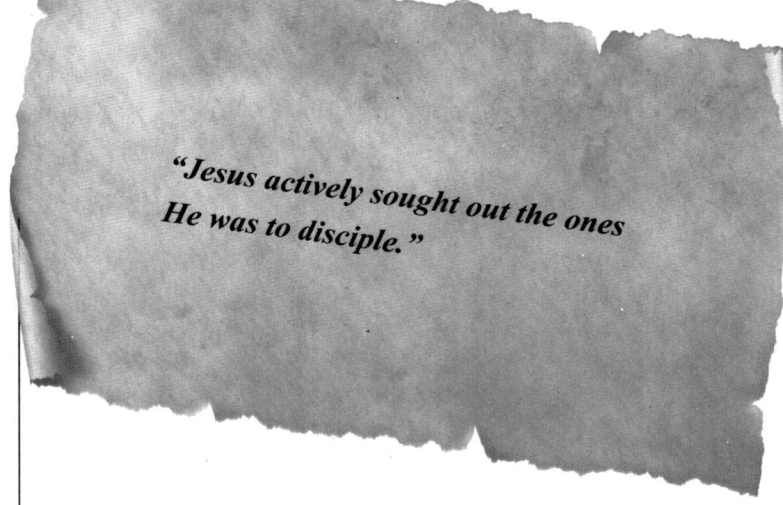

"Jesus actively sought out the ones He was to disciple."

*"Now before the Feast of the Passover, Jesus knowing that His hour had come that He would depart out of this world to the Father, **having loved His own who were in the world, He loved them to the end**."* John 13:1

Everything that 1 Corinthians 13:4-7 describes as the nature of love is how Jesus was to His disciples, and all of the Father's love was poured out through Jesus to them. Be sure to never stray from loving those you are discipling. Let your love be God's love toward them.

Where do I start?

For you to make disciples, you must first be a disciple yourself. So, you must make time to be discipled by Jesus. You do this in the same way that you disciple someone else, by spending one-on-one time with your Lord and Teacher. To start, carve out time each day to be alone in studying the Word and in prayer, worship, and fellowship with Him. To do this, you may need to rearrange your schedule or cut out a commitment or two. You may be doing a lot of good work and many important things, so this is where you need to make some tough decisions, understand what is priority, and start rearranging your life to make time for Jesus. Let the Holy Spirit help you; pray and ask Him for guidance. You don't need "discipleship training" to start discipling someone. All it takes is for you to have an active relationship with Jesus!

Once you have a solid routine of being in relationship with Jesus, ask the Holy Spirit for someone to disciple. Then go and seek out some people! It's simple - find someone you like and connect with them. Ask them out for breakfast, lunch, or dinner sometime. How about grabbing a coffee sometime? Maybe a phone call or video chat. Or a bike ride, a run, a walk in the park, crafts, baking, or whatever fits your fancy. Just hang out for a while. See where it goes. Not everyone is going to be receptive to a deep relationship, and that's okay - some people are just not there yet in their level of openness. So, move on to the next person.

It may be easier and more logical to seek those younger than you to disciple, but it doesn't have to be that way. Many people are not born again until later in life and need to be discipled by someone who knows just a little more than they do to help them grow in their relationship with Jesus. This also doesn't have to be a believer you are to disciple. It could be a non-believer that doesn't go to church. As Jesus is praying for His disciples in John 17, He says in verse 18, *"As You sent Me into the world, I also have sent them into the world."* He has done the same for us today. As His disciples, we are to go out into the world - yes, in the filth and muck of the world - and build relationships with those of the world with the intention of discipling them. You might get a little dirty; you may get a little uncomfortable, but that's okay - people work is messy work. This could be a co-worker, a friend of a friend, someone you know through a sport or other organization, or a neighbor. If a non-believer is open to you, and it can be a healthy relationship, then disciple them to Jesus, and continue to disciple them as they mature as a follower of Jesus.

Now that you've found someone you connect with, continue to fellowship with that person and love them. Genuine love and grace change a person. Focus on them and care about them. This is going to start as two people enjoying their time together and maybe not even talking about the Bible or spiritual things at first. Make it regular and consistent. If it's a true relationship, that person will also make the effort because they are benefiting from your discipling them, and enjoying that time with you. This is actually a mutually beneficial relationship. You will benefit from discipling someone just as much they are benefiting from your discipling them.

Then, simply be yourself. Be genuine. You are a likable and wonderful person! Listen to them first, but eventually share the wisdom you've gained throughout your life so they can learn from you. Also, share with them new insights and revelations you receive from the Holy Spirit, both from the Word of God and about life. These are treasures in you that are meant to be given, just as Jesus tells His disciples in Matthew 13:52:

"He said to them, Therefore every teacher and interpreter of the Sacred Writings who has been instructed about and trained for the kingdom of heaven and has become a disciple is like a householder who brings forth out of his storehouse treasure that is new and [treasure that is] old [the fresh as well as the familiar]." (AMPC)

You have been instructed and trained for the kingdom of heaven and have a storehouse full of treasures in you, so share what you have!

Remember this as well; Jesus is in you, so He *will* come out of you. You are being discipled by Jesus and, as a result, are being changed into His likeness. So what proceeds from you to the person you are discipling is everything you've received from Jesus: patience, joy, kindness, grace, encouragement, gentleness, peace, a sense of safety, and, most importantly, unconditional love.

If you are a new or young believer, it would be good for you to find a trustworthy, mature follower of Jesus interested in having a friendship with you that could also disciple you. Use the same advice (as shared above) to start that relationship. Hopefully, someone will reach out to you along the way. If not, you'll have to do some seeking yourself, and it may require you to outright ask someone to disciple you. Pray and trust in the Lord that He will bring someone to you - He will.

I would encourage *any* person to be discipled by another more mature believer while you are also discipling others. This is the kind of connection and bond Jesus had in mind for His church. Listen to what Jesus says in John 14:34-35:

"A new commandment I give to you, that you love one another; as I have loved you, that you also love one another. By this all will know that you are My disciples, if you have love for one another.

Being discipled and discipling others is demonstrated love for one another. It shows the world we are *all* disciples of Jesus.

You are not alone

Take note of the last thing that Jesus says in His Great Commission to us: *I am with you always.* This discipling thing may be new territory for you, and if you've never been discipled or mentored yourself, it's completely foreign. You may think, "What do I have to give?" If you have some life experience under your belt and a relationship with Jesus, you have *a lot* to give! You may not realize the wisdom you possess, but it's gold to the youngsters today who are just starting life out in the world. Don't be fooled. The internet doesn't have all the answers. Relationships are what is missing. It's a step of obedience - Jesus will give you all you need to disciple someone. Listen to the words of Jesus in John 20:21-22 after His resurrection when He appeared to His disciples:

"Peace be with you; as the Father has sent Me, I also send you." And when He had said this, He breathed on them and said to them, "Receive the Holy Spirit."

Just as the Father sent Jesus and was with Jesus during His ministry on earth, so Jesus is with you and has sent you out into the world. He's not going to send you out without supplying you with all you need. Notice Jesus gives the Holy Spirit. Be baptized with the Holy Spirit and walk in His power as you disciple! Don't do this in your own power; you will fail. Then give Jesus all the credit for the impact you have on the people you disciple. Jesus is ultimately the one who changes people, not us.

But...

"...I'm too busy. I don't have time."
"...I'm not good at starting relationships."
"...I have enough friends."
"...I'm not qualified."
"...I don't know how. I've never done it before."

There are many reasons to avoid discipling others, and they are all valid. I've used many of these excuses myself. What I have determined in my mind, however, is, "NO EXCUSES! I *need* to do this!" Discipling others is too important to pass it off as just another demand from the church or just one more thing we need to do as Christians. This is not only a command of Jesus but also the heart of Jesus. The entire time of His ministry on this earth, He was discipling others and building close relationships. Discipling others is very dear to Jesus, and it's the most effective way to advance His Kingdom. We need to make it a priority.

Our modern society is extremely demanding, and we are all so busy. You may need to step back and evaluate where your time is going and let some things go. I understand it may not be easy; you are doing a lot of good things. So you may have to replace a "good" to do the "greater."

Side note: Parents of young ones - it's a busy time in life, and your family comes first. Good news, you are discipling your children! (Yes, that counts.) It can be challenging, but still try to find time to spend with the Lord regularly. Then put immense effort into raising your children to be vibrant disciples of Jesus.

Action steps

1. If you are not doing this already, determine to spend alone time studying the Word of God and in prayer regularly. Think right now about how you can rearrange your day or week to make this happen.

2. Right now, think of one person you could contact that you could disciple. This could be a co-worker, a current friend of yours, someone you go to church with, a friend's son or daughter, a cousin - anybody! If you cannot think of someone, take time right now to ask the Lord who that person could be. The same is true if you are looking for someone to disciple you. Think of a couple of people just in case the first one doesn't work.

3. Make a reminder for yourself to contact that person to get together or contact them right now. Don't give up on this. Keep going until you find someone to disciple or a person to disciple you.

That's it! You're going to love it! It's good for you, it's good for the world, and it glorifies God. Go!

Jeremy lives in rural Fulton County, Ohio, with his wife and daughter. Driven by his passion for the Word, he seeks to advance the Kingdom where he is as he works in the IT industry.

The Blessing of Christ...Obtaining His Fullest

By Denise Emerine

"I am sure that when I come to you, I shall come in the fullness of the blessing of the gospel of Christ." (Romans 15:29). Paul wrote these words to the Christians in Rome. He was telling them, "I have no doubt that when I meet you, it will be in the *fullest measure* of Christ's blessing."

The apostle's words here imply something that every believer must know. That is, there are various degrees, or measures, of Christ's blessing. Some believers obtain a full measure of this blessing, which is the goal. We're all meant to come into a full measure of the Lord's blessing. Yet other Christians enter into only a small measure of Christ's blessing.

In his letter to the Ephesians, Paul urges everyone to pursue the fullest measure of this blessing: *"Unto every one of us is given grace according to the measure of the gift of Christ... Till we all come in the unity of the faith, and of the knowledge of the Son of God, unto a perfect man, unto the measure of the stature of the fullness of Christ... To know the love of Christ, which surpasses knowledge, that you might be filled with all the fullness of God"* (Ephesians 4:7, 13, 3:19).

Note the word "fullness" in these passages. The Greek word Paul uses here means "to complete the task of filling up to full." That is the task God has given us: to pursue the fullness of Christ's blessing in our lives.

Paul elaborates on this, writing, "There is … one LORD, one FAITH, one BAPTISM, one GOD and FATHER of all, who is above all and through all, and in you all" (Ephesians 4:4-6). In short, God the Father, Son, and Holy Spirit abides in all His children. Jesus promised, *"We will come and make our abode in you"* (see John 14:23). Paul is making clear that we all have the same access to the LORD. Therefore, we all have equal opportunity to obtain His ever-increasing blessing. Indeed, our lives should continually increase in what Paul calls "the blessing of Christ.'

Consider the incredible measure of Christ's blessing in Paul's life. This man received revelations from Jesus personally. He writes that Christ revealed Himself in him. Of course, Paul knew he hadn't attained perfection. He also knew, without a doubt, that there was nothing in his life hindering the flow of Christ's blessing.

This is why Paul could say, *"I am sure that when I come to you, I shall come in the fullness of the blessing of the gospel of Christ"* (Romans 15:29). He had a holy confidence in his walk with Christ. He claims, *"Herein do I exercise myself, to have always a conscience void of offense toward God, and toward men"* (Acts 24:16).

Paul was saying, in essence, "My life is an open book before the LORD. I have no hidden sin in my heart, and he has no controversy with me. And His blessing to me is a continuous flow of revelation. So, when I preach to you, you don't hear the words of men. I don't deliver a dead sermon full of clever theology. What you hear are the very words of God's heart to you."

You see, the fullness of Christ's blessing has little to do with material goods. Of course, all good health and earthly resources must be seen as blessings from God's gracious hand. However, Paul is speaking of a much greater blessing here. The Greek word he uses for blessing means "God's commendation" or His "Well done."

In short, the blessing of Christ means having a life that's pleasing to the Lord. It's an inner knowing from Holy Spirit that as God looks on your life, He says, "I'm pleased with you, my son, and my daughter. There is nothing between us to hinder our communion and relationship."

The writer of Hebrews sums up the fullness of Christ's blessing this way: *"The God peace, that brought again from the dead our Lord Jesus, that great Shepherd of the sheep, through the blood of the everlasting covenant, make you perfect in every good work to do His will, working in you that which is well-pleasing in His sight, through Jesus Christ; to whom be glory forever and ever"* (Hebrews 13:20-21).

I love being around people who live this kind of Christ life. They have about them the aroma of having been with Christ. Like Paul, these saints have a divine dissatisfaction with this life, a longing to be in the presence of Christ, a hunger to obtain more and more intimacy with Him. They speak much of Jesus, and they exude His love and holiness.

Such people enjoy life, but they avoid all foolish conversation. They live wholly separated from things of this world. And God's favor is evident in their lives and in their families. They may be poor, but their lives are fully blessed by the Lord.

Don't get me wrong: these believers suffer like everyone else. They go through seasons of severe trials and testing. Like Paul, although they may be cast down, they are not destroyed. They never quit! They're determined to finish their walk of faith and ministry in a way that's pleasing to God.

Paul asked the Galatians, "*You ran well: Who hindered you from obeying the truth? This persuasion does not come from Him who calls you. A little leaven leavens the whole lump*" (Galatians 5:7-9).

Paul is referring here to a mindset, a doctrinal belief, or theology. He's asking, "What's in your life that keeps you from going on in the full blessing of Christ? You were doing well at one time. I know you to be a praying people, and you labor diligently to do good works. But something's wrong. I don't see you growing anymore. Instead, you've gone back to relying on your flesh. I don't sense the sweet aroma of Christ you once had. Your certainty, your clarity, your vision, are gone. Something's hindering you.

"What could have persuaded you to settle in this condition? Whatever it is, I tell you it's not of God. In fact, I sense leaven in you, a compromise of some kind. Something is clouding you, something you may be holding onto, which is causing the Lord to have a controversy with you. Tell me, what is it?"

I know so many Christians today who once were mightily used of God. These people were devoted, praying, believing saints. Then something happened to them. Somehow, they were hindered from experiencing the fullness of the blessing of Christ.

This includes many ministers I know. These men saw victory after victory in their walk with the Lord. However, something crept into their lives, some compromise, and over time, they made peace with it. Often, that hindering leaven was a single besetting sin.

To all such people, Paul asks, "What happened? What's hindering the flow of Christ's blessing in your life? What leaven has crept in?"

The prophet Elijah was mightily used of God. He shared God's burden of grief over Israel. His heart broke over the people's backsliding. He performed great miracles and wonders in God's name. Yet, just as Moses was prevented from entering the Promised Land, Elijah was hindered from experiencing the complete fullness of God's blessing.

You know the story of Elijah's victory on Mount Carmel. The godly prophet called down fire from heaven and slew the prophets of Baal. Then he prayed for rain, and showers poured down, ending the long drought in Israel. When the people saw these things, they immediately repented of their idolatry and turned back to the Lord.

I want to pick up the story as the people started for Jezreel, the capital, to report the news. Incredibly, Elijah outran a speeding chariot to the city, a distance of over twenty miles! Scripture says, "*The hand of the Lord was upon Elijah*" (1 Kings 18:46) as he raced along. This tells me Elijah was on a divine mission. "The hand of the Lord" indicates His leading. God was sending Elijah back to Jezreel for a purpose. Why, exactly, was the prophet being hurried back to the capital?

We find a clue in Elijah's testimony at Mount Carmel: "*I have done all those things at His word*" (1 Kings 18:36). The prophet was saying, in essence, "Lord, let everyone here today know that everything I do is in submission to Your leading. What I've done here today is simply what You told me to do in prayer.

Then, wicked Queen Jezebel got the news. When she heard that Elijah had slain all her false prophets, she threatened to kill him. Scripture says, "*[King] Ahab told Jezebel all that Elijah had done, and how he had slain all the prophets with the sword. Then Jezebel sent a messenger to Elijah, saying, so let the gods do to me, and more also, if I do not make your life as the life of one of them by tomorrow about this time. And when he saw that, he arose and ran for his life, and went to Beersheba, which belongs to Judah, and left his servant there.*" (1 Kings 19:1-3)

Many Bible commentators believe Elijah wasn't afraid of Jezebel. They say his mission was fulfilled at Mount Carmel and that now God was leading him into the wilderness to teach him some important lessons. In other words, the Lord never intended for Elijah to face Jezebel back at Jezreel. I disagree. I think this interpretation misses the point of this passage entirely. As I picture bold Elijah racing back to Jezreel, I believe he was on his way to accomplish the one final thing that God had asked of him: to kill Jezebel.

Think about it: the Lord wasn't about to allow Jezebel to raise up a whole new corps of wicked priests. Why would God tell Elijah to slay her 400 prophets but allow the mother of idolatry to survive? It would be like lopping off sin's branches but allowing its roots to survive. When God prepares His people to enter the fullness of His blessing, He also calls us to root out our sin so that we can be brought into a life of purity and holiness. Only then can we experience His fullness.

I believe the Bible proves Jezebel had to be cut down. In Revelation, Jesus instructs the church in Thyatira, "I know your works, love, service, faith, and your patience; and as for your works, the last are more than the first. Nevertheless, I have this against you: because you allow that woman Jezebel, who calls herself a prophetess, to teach and seduce My servants to commit sexual immorality and to eat things sacrificed to idols… *"Behold, I will cast her into a bed, and those that commit adultery with her into great tribulation, except they repent of their deeds. And I will kill her children with death; and all the churches shall know that I am He who searches the minds and hearts. And I will give to each one of you according to your works"* (Revelation 2:19-23).

Christ is speaking here to a people who are charitable, full of faith, patient, growing in deeds. Yet these devoted saints still didn't have the Lord's full blessing. Why? Jesus tells them. "There is one issue, one hindrance that keeps you from experiencing my favor in full. That is, you refuse to deal with the Jezebel spirit in your midst. You allow that wicked spirit to go on seducing you." Christ makes it absolutely clear: if we are to enter into His fullness, we must get to the root of all idolatry and sin. So, what is the sin that Jezebel represents? Jezebel is a symbolic name. In Hebrew, it means "chaste?" with an intentional question mark. This suggests surprise at the very thought of chasteness – meaning, "certainly not chaste, not pure; that which is clearly impure." In short, Jezebel is a spirit of gross uncleanness and lust.

Some commentators don't believe Jezebel was the actual name of Ahab's wife. Rather, they say the writer used the name as a degrading epithet because of the queen's hated behavior. This was a common practice among biblical writers. For example, John uses the word "antichrist" not just to describe the person who's to come but also a spirit. The same is true with the use of "dragon." It's used to describe not only Satan but any entity that's controlled by him, including humans. Simply put, Jezebel is a seductive propaganda from hell, and it's aimed solely at God's servants. It's meant to bring down and destroy all who have been touched and anointed by the Lord. The passage on Mount Carmel bears this out. Have you ever wondered where those prophets of Baal come from? They weren't some imported immigrant priests. They were Israelites. God's chosen. They'd been seduced by Jezebel and led into fornication through devilish indoctrination.

There's no question in my mind Elijah was called to be an instrument to pull down that stronghold in Israel. Elijah had a history with the Lord and was trained to hear God's voice. He prayed with such power that the heavens were shut and opened again. When he struck a river with his mantle, the waters divided. Also, he raised a young boy from the dead. Elijah clearly lived and moved in the miraculous. He had once declared to Ahab with authority, "Elijah is here!" What courage! What fearlessness! Yet the mighty prophet was now running away in fear.

This same battle is being waged in God's house even now. Think of a devoted Christian, someone like Elijah. He's dedicated to God's work, diligent, patient, walking by faith, serving others, and increasing in good works, but there is a hindrance in his life. This servant has a measure of Christ: he's saved, justified, and occupied with the Father's business. Yet now the Lord comes to him, saying, "I have this against you. You've allowed something destructive in your life. A Jezebel spirit has seduced you. It's hindering you in your walk with Me." Jesus is speaking of those things you let indoctrinate you: TV, the Internet, Facebook, Twitter, and other lusts of the eyes and heart of the flesh. These are just a few, but all are powerful seducers.

Likewise, when Christ speaks of "eating things sacrificed to idols," he's not talking about food. He's referring to Christians who dine on the devil's filth. These believers may raise their voices in praise at church, but when they go home, they turn their minds to worthless things of the unimaginable: pornography, vulgar magazines and movies, TV shows that are sexual in nature, murders, cultish, violent, and abominations unto God. Even the world acknowledges the evil of such things.

Often, when the Jezebel spirit comes to seduce us, it whispers, "You've worked so hard, and now you need to relax. It's time you allowed yourself some recreation. This is the day of grace, and God isn't hard on His people. Go ahead, tune into that off-color TV show. Rent that racy movie; "we will just fast-forward through the bad parts." If you give a little more each time or indulge too much, you can always claim the blood of Jesus and get clean again."

No! Jesus says if you lust in your heart, you've already committed adultery. He tells us plainly, with flaming eyes, *"I gave her space to repent of her fornication; and she repented not"* (Revelation 2:21). The "her" in this verse signifies the deceived children of God, those seduced by Jezebel spirit.

The Lord is saying, "I am merciful toward you, and I have been very patient. I've given you lots of time to repent and forsake your sin. I have sent prophets to you, sermons from the pulpit, and many warnings from your friends. My Spirit has convicted you and warned in love. But you still have not repented. "I long for you to enter My fullness. I've laid out every resource before you. Yet, you continue to live like no one is watching. I, the Lord, have a controversy against you, and it won't go away until you deal with these hindrances."

Jesus tells us what these consequences are:

- *"I will cast her into a bed"* (Revelation 2:22). The Greek translation here is "wear down, put to flight." It signifies continual fear, weariness, always running.

- *"Great tribulation"* (2:22). The Greek suggests pressure, troubles, depression.

- *"I will kill her children with death"* (2:23). Unless those who make a covenant with Jezebel repent, their end will be literal death.

Why does the Lord deal so severely with those who go to bed with Jezebel? It's because He wants this matter taken seriously by everyone who serves Him: *"All churches will know that I am He who searches the minds and hearts of men: and I will give to every one of you according to your works."* These are not the words of some Old Testament prophet. It's a warning from Jesus Christ Himself in this day of grace. He's telling us that each individual in My church has to know that Jezebel must be cast down.

Let's go back now to Elijah. I consider him to be one of the mightiest men of God in all of Scripture. Yet he allowed Jezebel to live. Elijah failed in his mission with no justification. What was the root of Elijah's failure? It was a lack of faith. Elijah ascribed more power to Jezebel than to God. Think about it: after his victory on Mount Carmel, there was revival in the land, conviction among the people, and widespread repentance. Jezebel had no power left. If she had tried to kill Elijah, then the people would have surrounded him in protection. Instead, when the threat came, Elijah lost faith in God. Are you getting the point of this message? The God who saved you - who has given you victories over sin - and provided miracles for you - has the same power to kill any Jezebel lust in you. He can destroy every stronghold, mortify every besetting sin, and deliver you from all power of the enemy.

Many struggling Christians think, "This habit in me is so strong, I'm overwhelmed. Where is the victory?" That's when the enemy whispers to them, "God doesn't hear you. You're not going to make it. In spite of all your prayers, you're to fail." Then the Lord answers, "No! No stronghold, no Jezebel spirit, will have dominion over you." Elijah did what many believers consider doing: he ran away. David writes of wanting to fly away to the desert like a bird. Jeremiah wished he had an isolated cottage, far away in the wilderness. Yet most Christians who "run away" never actually go anywhere. For them, it's a frame of mind, despair, to get away from their trial. Eventually, David concluded, "I will fear no evil." Elijah gave up the fight, and Jezebel lived on.

I believe Elijah's story reveals one of the greatest compassionate acts God has ever shown any fearful servant. Elijah ended up under a juniper tree in the wilderness, so depressed that he fell into a heavy sleep. The Lord sent an angel to wake him up and feed him with a cake and some water. So Elijah ate and drank, but he was still so depressed he went straight to sleep again. Once more, the angel woke him and fed him another meal. Then God spoke these kind words to his servant: *"Elijah, the journey is too much for you. Here, sit up and eat"* (see 1 Kings 19:7). He was saying, "Friend, you can't handle this alone. I'm with you." You see, God's love for Elijah was never in question. It was a merciful warning, and it applies to us today as well. He asked, "What are you doing here, Elijah?" Even though the Lord had forgiven Elijah, He wasn't going to sweep his problem under the rug. He loved him too much.

Elijah answered with an excuse, but God wouldn't accept it. Again, he asked, "Why are you here?" He was asking, in essence, "Why did you give up the fight, Elijah? Why did you resign from your ministry? Where did your weariness come from?" In the end, it appears that God accepted Elijah's resignation. The Lord said, in so many words, "I won't force you to go on, Elijah. But I'm going to anoint Jehu in your place. He's going to fulfill your mission by killing Jezebel."

The fact is, saints, if we want to quit, the Lord will allow it. He won't love us any less. He will simply allow us to go on living with our limited measure of Christ. Indeed, when the time came for Elijah to go home to the Lord, he was carried to heaven in a chariot of fire. He was a man greatly honored. Like Moses, who was prevented from entering the Promised Land, Elijah never entered the fullness of God's blessing. You may be able to say, "I don't have a problem with lust. I'm not a fornicator or an adulterer. Thank God I haven't been seduced by the Jezebel spirit. "I rejoice with you. However, for every believer who desires to enter fully into the blessing of Christ, an Elijah moment will surely come. You'll encounter the biggest, most overwhelming enemy you've ever faced. The Jezebel spirit will taunt you. "This time, you're going to fall. It's over for you."

"When that time comes, you cannot think of quitting. Don't give up the fight or forsake the promises God has given you."

When that time comes, you cannot think of quitting. Don't give up the fight or forsake the promises God has given you. Cast down that Jezebel spirit. The Lord says it has no power over you. Here is one final picture of God's mercy. Even though Elijah failed, the Lord gave His servant the final word. Scripture says Elijah prophesied. *"The dogs shall eat Jezebel by the wall of Jezreel"* (1 Kings 21:23). That is just what happened. Jezebel was slain on the very spot where Elijah had fled, and the dogs licked up her blood. God gave Elijah the last word.

Dear Saint, our Lord has made us more than conquerors. That is His final word on the subject. So, get up and fight for His Kingdom! Allow Him to lead you into the fullness of His blessing so you hear one day, "Well done, My son, and well done, My daughter."

Denise currently serves as the Director of the Greater Toledo House of Prayer and Hope Park Memorial to the Unborn. She works alongside business owners in establishing prayer rooms in companies in the US and Israel. She is partnered with companies in Texas to launch colleges to the biblical entrepreneurship principles as the GAP…Generals As Priests in the marketplace. When she's relaxing, she loves to be with her husband and family of ten beautiful grandchildren.

A Prophetic Word for 2024

From Jim Pinkelman

"Behold, the days are coming," says the Lord GOD, "That I will send a famine on the land, Not a famine of bread, Nor a thirst for water, But of hearing the words of the LORD." Amos 8:11

There is an unseen famine in the world today. The Word of the Lord is drying up and being replaced with dry river beds. Where is their wisdom in the land? Where is the gentle rain of My Word? The world seeks food and water, yet they find nothing that will satisfy. They grow more and more hungry. They fill their minds with the hollowness of the media. They put on clothes to cover their ugliness. They fill their stomachs with food that does not satisfy their hunger or thirst. They do now know what they need. You have the answer, My people. As I told the disciples, feed them. Teach them, cloth them with Kingdom things. You say you do not know how. Walk in My Spirit, and I will show you the way. Humble yourself, and you will see the way. The world is so desperate. Feed them.

Today, I Choose My Lord!

By Jean Magrum

Years ago, the phrase, "Today, I Choose Joy," set me free in my heart! I love joy, happiness, fun, laughter, cracking jokes in stressful times, smiling, bouncing with life, and my husband has always said that he fell in love with me because of my zest for life. I had lost this, so this phrase became mine! I even found a coffee mug with those words on it, bought it, and use it almost daily.

"A cheerful heart is good medicine…" Proverbs 17:22 (NIV)

I know I am not perfect and never will be until I enter His presence for eternity. The older I get, the more I long to crawl up in His lap, feel His arms around me, and hold me tightly. To be set free from life's struggles, pain, ailments, and hurts sounds perfect to me. I know, though, that my time is not completed this side of heaven yet. I still have a husband, adult children and their spouses, and "grands" to love and invest in. My greatest joy for the past 18 years, as most any grandparent will agree, is my grands. I love loving them. They bring me so much joy as I age, a design by God for sure. So, *today, I choose joy!*

How can one live in joy with the way life can be sometimes? I mean, really. When we are being bombarded with the enemy's arrows, how can we really be joyous? How can one rise above this and even smile? I struggle with this still today. I seem to become that pain or hurt. I seem to live offended. The hurts will not let me go, as if they are squeezing the life and breath right out of me.

I am finding that the key to not letting the enemy steal my joy is staying parked in my Lord's Word. It is only there that I find comfort, healing, and the strength to keep moving forward. Something starts brewing in me, something deep inside that only God can do. If I believe in His Word, which I do, I cannot stay stuck in the mire and muck I find myself in so often.

I am still learning and getting to know Him more so I can rely on Him without wavering. I have found that I must really get to know Him by digging into His Word. What does this look like for me and maybe for you? An experience I recalled with my son Craig, sheds some light on this for me.

Craig, a teen at the time, came home from school, and I could immediately tell something was not right. He came in the door, went to the sink to get a drink of water, and just by watching him do that, I could tell something was wrong.

I asked, "What's the matter, Craig?"

I will never forget his reaction. He spit his water out and said, thoroughly disgusted, "How do you do that?"

"Do what?" I asked seriously.

"How could you tell something was wrong? I made sure to hide it from you!" he said.

I smiled and said what came to me immediately. "I cannot have spent as much time as I have with you since birth and not 'know' you and know when something is wrong with you."

You see, I knew him because I had spent 17 years with him day in and day out. I lived in the trenches with him (and my daughters) and shared in their dreams, joys, accomplishments, struggles, sicknesses, and everything in between. How can one spend 24/7 with their children and not learn something along the way?

So, in truth, at that time, *I chose my children*. My dream career was getting married and raising a family, and I do not have a single regret. I learned who they were and how they ticked, and, along with my husband Mark, I invested all my time in them.

The same thing applies to my Lord. Do I start my day with Him faithfully as the most important One to give my time to, or do I just give Him a bit of time occasionally as I find the time? Do I seem just to fit Him into my busy schedule if I have nothing else better to do? I am a doer and like to get things done, and surely God understands because He made me this way. When I do sit down with Him, do I get distracted by devices around me? Does it seem that nothing is computing because my concentration is all over the place? Is He really my biggest priority each day? I have found that is the only way to really get to "know Him" and be able to then trust in Him fully. By the way, I am guilty of every one of those examples. I am a work in progress, but who isn't if we are truthful with ourselves?

"But if serving the LORD seems undesirable to you, then choose for yourselves this day whom you will serve…" Joshua 24:15 (NIV)

Who will I serve and obey today? Who will I trust today? Today and every day, Who or what will I choose? *Today, I choose my Lord.* For me, it must be a day-by-day decision.

Only then will I grow and learn Who my Lord is. Only then do I get to truly "know" Him and have a personal relationship with Him. Only then can I stand on His promises in faith without wavering because, you see, if I really "know" Him, I know I can trust Him and His promises. I am finding that in truly knowing Him, doubt flees. I can get angry with the enemy and stand against him. Jesus is His Word, so when we come to really know Him, it is not a struggle to stand in faith in His Word and His promises.

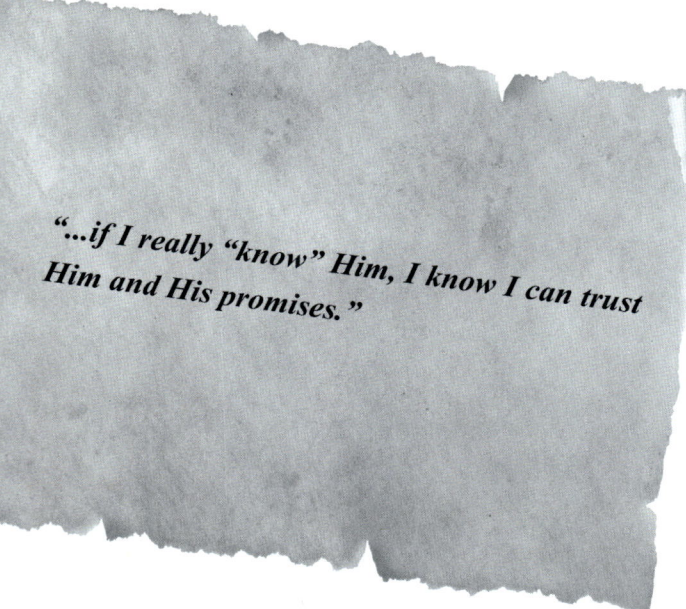

"...if I really "know" Him, I know I can trust Him and His promises."

"Now faith is the substance of things hoped for, the evidence of things not seen." Hebrews 11:1 (NKJV)

Faith in "what," or is it faith in "Whom"? Do I really walk by faith in my Lord and His promises, or do I let my head and heart be distracted by what I see? Maybe I just hope a person is healed. Is my faith in the healing or in my Lord?

I struggled so long with these verses: *"But let him ask in faith, with no doubting, for he who doubts is like a wave of the sea driven and tossed by the wind. For let not that man suppose that he will receive anything from the Lord; he is a double-minded man, unstable in all his ways."* James 1:6-8 (NKJV)

I cannot ask in faith if I do not "know" Him personally. If I only know about Him and His promises, without an intimate relationship, I will be double-minded and unstable, as Scripture states. I used to say, "I believe, I

believe, I believe," and then start doubting because I would walk by sight, not by faith. This is because I was hoping for the healing of the situation, not grounded on "Who" my Lord is, keeping my eyes on Him. He is not a magic lamp waiting to be rubbed for my next wish.

I hate seeing people sick, in pain, and beaten up by the enemy. It all started when a friend, who was doing some carpentry work in our home, tuned in to WJYM on our stereo in the afternoon. Between Godly programs and great announcers who invested in their listeners with Godly encouragement and truth, I started learning that the religion I was brought up in did not totally line up with God's Word. I became drawn to Truth and got saved, which started my journey of a relationship with my Lord.

A while after this, a dear friend of mine had a lot of serious health issues. Things just kept getting worse. While she was on a much-needed vacation with her husband out of state, she ended up in the hospital. I got so mad at the enemy. I prayed for healing for my friend. I even sent her a card encouraging her with Scripture verses on healing. I was stoked. I knew she would be healed because she, too, was a Christian.

A few days after I had mailed her that card to the hospital, her husband called and told me she had passed. I could not believe this! How could this be? Then I remembered the card I had mailed to her. The Scriptures I quoted and sent her did not come to pass. I panicked and needed to get that card back before her husband found it. Thankfully, the card was forwarded from the hospital to their home address, and I was retrieving his mail for him. When it arrived, I opened it, cried, and then threw it away. I guess you could also say I also threw out and walked away from this "healing" Jesus promises.

What I needed to learn yet was that healing is not about me and who I am but about God and Who He is. It is not that she was going to be healed, but we have His promise that we are healed. I did not yet understand Who He is and about His Kingdom promises to be able to stand and not waiver from His Truth.

"...who Himself bore our sins in His own body on the tree, that we, having died to sins, might live for righteousness—by whose stripes you were healed." 1 Peter 2:24 (NKJV)

In February 2009, my pastor and his wife started a Bible study. I started learning even more about Who my Lord really is, how much He loves me, wants His best for me, and created me to have a relationship with Him. I was finally growing, but seemingly not fast enough.

My husband Mark woke one December morning in 2009 with severe chest pains. I still shudder thinking about this. I should have been downstairs on the treadmill, but I had things to catch up on in the office first. God was guiding me without my even knowing. I was supposed to be in the office. Otherwise, I would never have heard Mark pounding on the wall, calling me for help.

When I went running to Mark, it was obvious he was having a heart attack. I called 911. They took what seemed forever to come. Tony, my son-in-law, even got there before the rescue squad. I was panicking, was all over the place emotionally, and could not pull myself together. I then asked Tony if he would pray over Mark, which he did. Tony spoke words of faith that Mark received. God's Word went before Mark!

It was two hours from when Mark woke in severe pain until his heart catheterization started and stents were inserted. The cardiologist found that the main artery to his heart, the left anterior descending artery, or the "widow maker" artery, was 100% blocked, along with other blockages. We also found out later that his organs had been shutting down by then, too. A few years later, paramedics told us while we were taking a CPR class that there is only a 12% chance of surviving a "widow maker" heart attack. God's Word is true. Mark's life is proof of this.

Then, in May 2019, Mark had some minor surgery. That night, when he woke, I noticed something was immediately wrong. I helped him out of bed and saw I had to call 911 again. Shortly after this, our son Craig was on the phone with me, and I asked Craig to pray over his Dad, which he did immediately. Craig spoke God's Word over Mark, and God's Word went before Mark again. Mark was rushed to the hospital, and while in the ER, Mark was not able to communicate with me. I flew out of that room to the nurse's station, told them what was going on, and within minutes, there were 8-10 people in that room attending to him.

Finally, they determined he was having a stroke. All we had to rely on was God. The next day, we also got the additional news that Mark had yet another heart attack. Our pastor helped us through this with encouragement and God's Word, and I can tell you today that Mark recovered from both the stroke and the 2nd heart attack very well. Thank You, Lord! We knew this was from God. Our faith continued to grow in Him and His Word.

I wish I could write that nothing more ever happened, but the enemy just loves to torment God's kids. In May of 2021, Mark was supposed to have a hip replaced, and I was not allowed back there with him when they were prepping him for surgery. They had just started prepping him when things went south immediately. A nurse came out to get me and asked me to go back with her to see Mark.

I said innocently, "I thought I wasn't allowed to go back there?"

She responded, "Well, he's having chest pains."

My heart sank. The nurse took me to the ER, where Mark had been transferred, but I could not get near him because of the many people attending to him. I sent a quick text to my kids and my pastor asking for prayer and why. Here I am in another emergency, and I reached out to others first instead of standing on God's Word first myself.

The text did not go through, as typically, there is no cell service in an ER area. I quickly realized it was just me, God and His Word, and Mark, though I still could not get near him. I had to suck it up and stand in my Lord alone, Who I know provided healing on the cross. I then got mad. The enemy was NOT going to steal my husband today! This is not what God had for Mark at all!

Within moments of this, God opened a pathway so that I could get to Mark. He was not doing well at all. I put my hand on his head and started speaking the Word into Mark's ear, not caring who else might be hearing me. Mark's life was in grave danger, and I could see that. I remember very clearly speaking God's Word to and over Mark, and then we both started praising God together while Mark was in such severe pain. That will never leave my heart.

A nurse at this hospital looked at me when they were getting ready to transport Mark to another hospital and said, "You are a strong woman. I can see that. You will be fine."

Inside, I was crumbling like never before, but when I heard those words, I looked back at her eyeball to eyeball and said, "I am. Thank you for reminding me of this." God provided this woman to encourage me when I surely needed it.

They tried to stabilize Mark and then sent him to another hospital where "the best open-heart surgeon" was ready to start open-heart surgery on another patient. Mark was placed ahead of this other person because Mark's condition was more immediately life-threatening.

Another heart catheterization showed Mark needed triple bypass surgery, and the main artery to his heart was again blocked 100%, along with two other arteries with severe blockage.

Mark's surgery took hours and hours but went well, thank You, Lord, again! Pastors Todd and Donna were able to join me at the hospital. Their loving support and encouragement compare to no one else I know.

When Mark's surgery was over, and I could see him, I was not fully prepared for what I was about to see. It truly was the hardest thing I have ever had to deal with. He was hooked up to every machine imaginable and was in a drug-induced coma. I prayed for him, held his hand, and cried a lot of tears. Mark was still here. God's Word is true, and He is faithful. I was looking at a true miracle man yet again. Our Lord continued to be faithful. Mark survived a 2nd widow maker's heart attack, and I do not even know if there are stats on surviving two of them.

I am happy to write that Mark recovered well again. Thank You, Lord! Do not ever try to tell me that God's Word is not true or that He is not faithful to His Word. Mark is living proof that it is. *That day, I chose the Truth of God's Word and trusted fully in my Lord!*

I have lost dear family members and friends to sickness and disease, but I am not going to second guess anything or wonder. While I do not understand everything in this life, I must return to this unequivocal truth, "My Lord is faithful." Because man chose disobedience to God, sickness and disease became one of the many results. We all must die someday unless Jesus returns first for His bride, but dying to sickness is not God's will, as Jesus provided so much for us on the cross, including healing.

What I have learned is that God wants us to fully love Him, which results in obedience to Him and His Word. To be able to be obedient to Him, though, I first must "know" Him. I cannot be obedient to just anyone. It must be Someone I fully trust, respect, love, and fear (absolute reverence, deep respect, and awe) and have a deep relationship with. God does not want just a surface relationship, but one where my heart connects with His, my heart is in tune with His, my steps are His, my will is what His will is, and I am obedient to Him and His Word. There is no more "Jean," thus dying to myself.

"My son, if you will receive my words and treasure my commandments within you, So that your ear is attentive to [skillful and godly] wisdom, And apply your heart to understanding [seeking it conscientiously and striving for it eagerly]; Yes, if you cry out for insight, And lift up your voice for understanding; If you seek skillful and godly wisdom as you would silver And search for her as you would hidden treasures; Then you will understand the [reverent] fear of the Lord [that is, worshiping Him and regarding Him as truly awesome] And discover the knowledge of God." Proverbs 2:1-5 (AMP)

Yesterday is over, so I can only repent and move on. I am not promised tomorrow, so what I am left with is today. What am I going to do today? What or Whom do I choose today? When the enemy attacks me through offense received from people, depression, or sickness, how do I choose to respond? I have a choice, as our loving Lord gave us free will. He created us to choose to love Him or not, be obedient to Him or not, and be one with Him or not. He wants us to genuinely love Him just like He loves us.

"But store up for yourselves treasures in heaven, where neither moth nor rust destroys, and where thieves do not break in and steal; for where your treasure is, there your heart [your wishes, your desires; that on which your life centers] will be also. Matthew 6:20-21 (AMP)

I finally realized that I was all too often speaking from the flesh instead of my spirit, so I had to just stop speaking.

"Stand silent! Know that I am God!" Psalm 46:10 (TLB)

I started evaluating my thoughts in my head, thinking about what I was going to say before I spoke. It was humbling, to say the least. I have so much junk in my head and heart that I would have never believed otherwise. It was only then that I could listen to my precious Holy Spirit. Once I started getting myself out of the way, the Holy Spirit could press upon my heart His way, His Words, and His choices for me. Trust me, it was not easy, but oh so freeing! I was not obeying my Lord but living in and justifying my wounds. "Things were not my fault!" I would soothe myself, but how I respond to any situation is my fault if it is not my Lord's way. I cannot walk and be obedient to my Lord while licking my wounds in justification and living in my pain.

"Loving God means doing what he tells us to do, and really, that isn't hard at all; for every child of God can obey him, defeating sin and evil pleasure by trusting Christ to help him." 1 John 5:3-4 (TLB)

This verse is only possible if I "know" my Lord intimately. To truly love my Lord, I must be obedient to Him and His Word. I cannot justify my sin because of others. This is much easier once I know Whom I have chosen to trust. We were made to have a relationship with our Creator, and this relationship requires obedience, which takes faith, courage, and trust in my Lord.

"Teacher, which is the greatest commandment in the Law?" And Jesus replied to him, "'You shall love the Lord your God with all your heart, and with all your soul, and with all your mind.' This is the first and greatest commandment. The second is like it, 'You shall love your neighbor as yourself [that is, unselfishly seek the best or higher good for others].' The whole Law and the [writings of the] Prophets depend on these two commandments." Matthew 22:36-40 (AMP)

I have learned to never give up on myself and my relationship with my Lord. I can no longer put off time with my Lord because the result will be that I will stop growing. I must press on to my goal, which is walking in oneness with my Lord.

"We can rejoice, too, when we run into problems and trials, for we know that they are good for us—they help us learn to be patient. And patience develops strength of character in us and helps us trust God more each time we use it until finally our hope and faith are strong and steady. Then, when that happens, we are able to hold our heads high no matter what happens and know that all is well, for we know how dearly God loves us, and we feel this warm love everywhere within us because God has given us the Holy Spirit to fill our hearts with his love." Romans 5:3-5 (TLB)

I do not know the future or how my Lord might use me for His purpose, but I do know that I cannot be chasing just after the "things" of God. I was trying to stand on my Lord's Word without knowing Who He is. I must allow Him to direct my paths, to walk with me and talk with me, and His Word directing me. In Him, I submit my life, which means laying down my hurts, struggles, and failures at His feet, letting His blood wash over me and cleanse me, freeing me to grow more in Him each day. This frees me to be used by Him as He wishes and directs, not by me directing my Lord.

"Therefore I urge you, brothers and sisters, by the mercies of God, to present your bodies [dedicating all of yourselves, set apart] as a living sacrifice, holy and well-pleasing to God, which is your rational (logical, intelligent) act of worship. And do not be conformed to this world [any longer with its superficial values and customs], but be transformed and progressively changed [as you mature spiritually] by the renewing of your mind [focusing on godly values and ethical attitudes], so that you may prove [for yourselves] what the will of God is, that which is good and acceptable and perfect [in His plan and purpose for you]. Romans 12:1-2 (AMP)

I know that this growth is building my faith, which is also improving my prayer life. When I need to just be with Him or am struggling with something, I default to my "go-to" with my Lord. I crank up my praise and worship music and just praise Him with everything in me. The enemy flees for sure and loses control over me!

A few people have told me, "It's in you, Jean! It is in you!" May I suggest it is in all of us? For me, Scripture verses are starting to come to my mind and heart any time of the day or night. I am getting so angry with the enemy and then using my authority that I have in my Jesus! There is a bubbling inside of me, which I know is from the Holy Spirit! It is exciting, to say the least!

After Jesus spent three years with His disciples, He stopped calling them His servants and then called them His friends. Why did their relationship change? It changed because His disciples kept pressing in to really know Him.

"You are my friends if you keep on doing what I command you. I do not call you servants any longer, for the servant does not know what his master is doing; but I have called you [My] friends, because I have revealed to you everything that I have heard from My Father." John 15:14-15 (AMP)

I want to be Jesus' friend, but more importantly, I want to be His obedient disciple, always learning, growing, and always serving Him first. I began by asking the question, "How can one live in joy with the way life can be sometimes?" My experiences have taught me to look to my Lord and keep pressing on in life and pressing in with Him, deciding not to let life steal anything from me, especially His unconditional love for me. This is my choice! I must search His Word with all my heart and never give up.

"Draw near to God and He will draw near to you." James 4:8 (NKJV)

Let Him love you each day. You have nothing to lose, I know. *Today, I Choose My Lord!*

Jean has been married to her husband, Mark, for almost 50 years. They have raised three amazing children who, along with their spouses, love serving the Lord. Mark and Jean have been blessed with eight grandchildren who are the joy of their lives. Jean gives her Lord all the glory for her marriage and family.

A Biblical Phrase for 2024
"It Came to Pass"

When we read "it came to pass" in the Bible, it merely sounds like a literary device to move us from one Biblical account to another. But every word and phrase in the Bible is placed with purposeful intent, bringing out powerful truth if we seek it. "It came to pass" occurs 20 times in the New Testament and about 150 times in the Old Testament.

In the New Testament, the phrase "it came to pass" is a translation of the Greek word "ginomai". It means to emerge and to transition from one point, realm, or condition to another. We see this word used when Jesus was baptized.

⁹ It came to pass in those days that Jesus came from Nazareth of Galilee, and was baptized by John in the Jordan. ¹⁰ And immediately, coming up from the water, He saw the heavens parting and the Spirit descending upon Him like a dove. ¹¹ Then a voice came from heaven, "You are My beloved Son, in whom I am well pleased." Mark 1:9-11 NKJV

He did emerge from the water and transitioned from one condition to another. Filled with the Holy Spirit, He transitioned into kingdom power and authority.

We saw that the phrase "It came to pass" means, in part, to "emerge and transition from one point, realm or condition to another." When Jesus emerged from the water, He transitioned into kingdom power and authority, allowing eternity to emerge through Him by the Holy Spirit.

We get a deeper understanding of the phrase when we understand the meaning of the Hebrew word that is translated as "it came to pass." That word is "vayehi." It has multiple layers of meaning but can be summarized by saying even when things look bad, something good will come from it. It is encapsulated in Joseph's words to his brothers in Genesis, when he said, "What you meant for evil, God meant for good."

As we walk through the year 2024, remember, "it came to pass." No matter what comes your way, never forget that what the enemy means for evil, Jesus turns to your good. And always be ready to transition into another realm, allowing the kingdom of God to manifest through you and your life to glorify the name of Jesus.

Institutional Teaching

By Jeff Millslagle

"…by far, the best way to learn from a Bible teacher is to personally sit under their teaching. It is one of the best reasons to go to church as opposed to watching a service online."

The teaching of the Scriptures has always been instrumental to the growth of individuals following the LORD. While it is true anyone can read and study the Bible individually, there is an unparalleled and vital role of having the Scriptures taught to us. This teaching of the Word allows us to gain the benefit from the study of others, thereby enabling us to supplement our own study. It broadens our understanding of the text. It helps bring clarity to passages of Scripture we may find difficult. Often referred to as "being fed," having the Bible taught to you by a solid, well-trained, gifted Bible expositor is a personally refreshing experience. This should never take the place of personal study, but individual time in the Word is greatly enhanced by sitting under Bible teachers. While this teaching can be experienced through various forms of media – radio, television, books, video clips, etc. – by far, the best way to learn from a Bible teacher is to personally sit under their teaching. It is one of the best reasons to go to church as opposed to watching a service online.

While fellowship with other believers and corporate worship (singing, prayer, communion, etc.) are all valid, essential, and important reasons we gather as a church body, it is the teaching of the Word which is the pre-eminent activity. Bible teaching – or preaching, if you prefer – should be the major focus of a church Sunday gathering you attend.

By the time of the earthly ministry of Jesus, small gatherings of Jewish people would meet at a synagogue in their community where portions of the Torah were read and expounded upon. We read this in Luke chapter 4 where Jesus went into the synagogue in Nazareth to read publicly from the Torah. In the Book of Acts, Peter and Paul would speak to large groups of people. We often speak of the 1st-century churches of Ephesus, Rome, Corinth, Philippi, etc. For many people, the concept of sitting under a person teaching the Scriptures may seem like a New Testament concept. But the public gathering of people to hear the Word of God taught to them goes back to the early times of Israel. I'm defining this exercise as "Institutional Teaching," which I believe sets the stage for our modern activity of sitting under a Bible teacher who explains passages of Scripture. Sitting under the teaching of the Word of God is not a New Testament concept. It is as old as the nation of Israel itself.

The Scripture is full of various examples of times when teaching or instruction in the Law was made a priority. From Moses to the time of Nehemiah, the Law (the Old Testament) played a major role in the success of the nation. When there was an intentional thrust of exposing the people to God's Word, the nation seemed to thrive. When it was neglected, the people and the nation found themselves worshipping pagan gods; they often were devoid of healthy leadership, and they faced overwhelming hardship and experienced disaster.

We, too, tend to ride a wave of spiritual success or failure based partially on our diligence to sit under or learn from quality Bible teaching. It helps balance our personal theology and allows us to glean wisdom from others, and supplements our personal study. Further, the writer of Hebrews tells us we are not to neglect the "assembling of ourselves together" (Hebrews 10:25). The regular gathering of believers for fellowship, worship, and – what I consider the most vital aspect of church – Bible teaching, is critical for the spiritual growth of any believer.

Looking at some of the many examples of Institutional Teaching in the Old Testament, we can better grasp the importance of Bible teaching for the spiritual advancement of those who claim the name of Jesus.

Moses

From the very beginnings of Israel, instruction from the Word of God was part of their life. Not long after the Exodus from Egypt, we read how Moses "told the people all the words of the LORD and all the judgments" (Exodus 24:3). However, this couldn't have been the first time the people had received instruction of some degree. In Exodus chapter 1, the midwives, who were commanded by the king of Egypt to kill any male babies, "feared the LORD and did not do what the king commanded them" (Exodus 1:17). Even before the formal declaration of the leadership of Moses, there had to have been some direction given the people by their leaders whereby those midwives knew it would be wrong before God to honor the king's command. Even in Israel's earliest days, instruction, whether formal or not, must have been part of their lives. Of course, after the Exodus, Moses rose to the position of leader of the people, and he instructed them in God's Laws.

While the Books of Exodus and Leviticus introduce the Law, a considerable amount of Deuteronomy is Moses reminding them of their history and repeating large portions of the Law for the people. This seems to occur close to the end of the life and leadership of Moses. By now, Moses was the aged, wise sage of Israel. Before the children of Israel entered the Promised Land, he gave them a reminder of where they came from, how they arrived there, and the Laws of God they were to follow as a people.

"On this side of the Jordan in the land of Moab, Moses began to explain this law..." – Deuteronomy 1:5

Moses begins a long message to the people. This group of people had not experienced firsthand God's deliverance from Egypt or the miracle of the Red Sea crossing. This is the subsequent generation who had to be taught of God's ways; they needed to be reminded of their history.

"And Moses called all Israel, and said to them: "Hear, O Israel, the statutes and judgments which I speak in your hearing today, that you may learn them and be careful to observe them." – Deuteronomy 5:1

No less than 40 times, God instructs Moses to "speak to the children of Israel" various instructions. These commands, along with reminders of their history, made up the bulk of their law. Everyone was to hear these instructions and learn from them. These were to be foundational to their culture as a people.

In Deuteronomy 11, Moses commanded them to write down the blessings and put them on Mt. Gerizim, and the curses would be put on Mt. Ebal (Deuteronomy 11:29). Later, in chapter 27, a ceremony is described where the law was written out for them. Six tribes would stand on each mountain, and the blessings and curses would be recited publicly. This instruction was carried out in Joshua 8. After writing the law on "whole stones" (verse 31), the law was read to them (verse 34). The event is summed up in verse 35.

"There was not a word of all that Moses had commanded which Joshua did not read before all the assembly of Israel, with the women, the little ones, and the strangers who were living among them" – Joshua 8:35

God wanted His people to know His Word, and with Joshua replacing Moses, the instruction of God's Word to the people would continue. This would have been particularly important in this early life of the nation as they needed clear instructions concerning the things of the LORD. God had moved in a mighty way, and now, decades removed from their lives of bondage, keeping them focused on the ways of God, they needed to be reminded of their history. They were a group of people dedicated to following God, and strong institutional teaching played a vital role in their survival as a nation.

After the death of Joshua, there is scant reference to the "Law of Moses" or the Word or Commandments of the LORD until the monarchy. Within Scripture, there is no mention of the law after Joshua 24:26 until the time of David. The Ark of the Covenant makes only a brief appearance in Judges 20 and isn't mentioned prominently until 1 Samuel. The death of Joshua created a vacuum of leadership that neglected any focus on the instruction of the Word of God to the people.

Kings David and Solomon

When David appears on the scene in 1 Samuel 16, the Law plays more of a prominent role in the life of Israel. David, of course, wrote many of the Psalms, and it is reasonable to conclude these were spoken or sung over the people as they worshipped, especially after the Ark returned to Jerusalem. One of David's worship leaders, Asaph, put many of David's Psalms to music and conducted their performance in worship (1 Chronicles 16:5, 7, 37). Asaph seems to have formed a sort of musical guild which took the title "The Sons of Asaph," which continued in some form through the post-exilic time of Ezra and Nehemiah (Ezra 3:10 and Nehemiah 11:17). This group followed Asaph's lead as he "prophesied according to the order of the king" (1 Chronicles 25:1-2). He also wrote various Psalms, notably Psalms 50 and 73-82.

Since many of David's psalms, along with Asaph's, were put to music, it is possible for one to conclude Scripture, and in particular, many Psalms were sung publicly. Perhaps many of those were expanded upon and taught as the singers were learning the words of the songs, particularly during the reigns of David and Solomon. King David's son Solomon built the temple, and Asaph (or his musical guild) was featured in the temple's dedication service singing this often-used line from various Psalms, "For He is good, For His mercies endure forever" (2 Chronicles 5:12-13).

Yet, there is no mention of the Law being taught to the people. They were to obey the law and offer sacrifices "according to all that is written in the Law" (1 Chronicles 16:40), but it would seem there was little or no emphasis put into public or Institutional teaching, beyond the singing of various Psalms.

Of course, David and his son Solomon were kings who followed the law, flawed men as they were, and it is reasonable to believe they encouraged the reading and teaching of the Law within the nation. Both of those men sought after the LORD and His Word. Near the time of King David's death, he gave some final advice to Solomon, instructing him to "…walk in His (the LORD's) ways, to keep His statutes…as it is written in the Law of Moses" (1 Kings 2:2).

At the dedication of the newly built temple, King Solomon refers to the promises of God and the Torah. He said, "There has not failed one word of all His good promise which He promised through His servant Moses" (1 Kings 9:56). When Solomon mentions "His servant Moses" he is, of course, referring to the Law. Yet, it would seem their celebration of the completed project did not include any reading or teaching of the Law. The temple, not the Law, was the focal point of the reign of Solomon. Years later, Solomon violated various warnings of the Law as he began to "love many foreign women" (1 Kings 11:1). In verse 3 of 1 Kings 11, he is said to have "clung to these in love." The Law was no longer the love of his life, and in his last years, he wasn't the Godly king he had been as he began his reign.

Kings Asa and Jehoshaphat

After the reigns of David and Solomon, succeeding generations did not seem to place any importance on seeking God and following the Law. It wasn't until King Asa, the great-grandson of Solomon, that Judah once again had a king who sought after the LORD. In 2 Chronicles 15, there is a prophet named Azariah who spoke with the king. Describing the chaos of the time of the Judges and the reigns of Rehoboam and Abijah – the grandfather and father of King Asa – the prophet encouraged the king. He told him, "The LORD is with you" (2 Chronicles 15:2). Then the prophet said:

> *"For a long time Israel has **priest**, and without law; but when in their trouble they turned to the LORD God of Israel, and sought Him, He was found by them. And in those times there was no peace to the one who went out, nor to the one who came in, but great turmoil was on all the inhabitants of the lands."*
> *- 2 Chronicles 5:3-5 (emphasis mine)*

From this passage, it's reasonable to conclude there had been "teaching priests" in Israel in the past. However, at this point, the teaching of the Law did not seem to have been a priority in the nation. As a result, the nation itself faltered and was often under oppression by outside forces. While the text does not directly indicate the king instilled a public teaching policy, he did gather the people together and renewed a covenant with the LORD (2 Chronicles 15:12). For most of his long reign, there was peace in the land.

In his last few years, King Asa grew prideful and would not submit to the LORD's discipline. Due to his allegiance with

Syria, he became "diseased in his feet," as indicated in 2 Chronicles 16:12. While Asa ranks as a good king of Israel, his final years cast a shadow on his reign. Is it possible, just as there had been in King Solomon's reign, there was a lack of emphasis upon the teaching of the law in his later years while he allowed pride to corrupt his mind?

Some scholars believe it is possible the king's son, Jehoshaphat, co-reigned with his father in his last years. Having an infirmity that may have hindered his mobility, the king may not have been able to perform many public functions. It is reasonable to conclude his son may have been required to function in his stead. It is also likely that Jehoshaphat realized some of his father's shortcomings which may have been a result of the Law not being taught to the people. Therefore, once he became King, he made a point to walk "in the former ways of his father David," and he "walked in His Commandments" (2 Chronicles 17:3-4). King David – not his father, King Asa – served as a role model for his reign. David was a man of God's Word and delighted in His Word. The same is said of King Jehoshaphat. In 2 Chronicles 17:6, we are told how the king, "took delight in the ways of the LORD."

Jehoshaphat developed an intentional program for the public teaching of the Law. As described in verse 7 of 2 Chronicles 17, he sent five of his "leaders" to "teach in the cities of Judah." This occurred during the third year of his reign and therefore indicates the high priority he placed on the teaching of the Law. This importance is further indicated by how widespread this teaching regimen was enforced.

> *"So they taught in Judah and had the Book of the Law of the LORD with them; they went throughout all the cities of Judah and taught the people."*
> *– 2 Chronicles 17:9*

Jehoshaphat wasn't just interested in exercising power as a king, but he wanted the people to know the Law. This intentional instruction in the Word had a profound impact on the people during his long reign.

After an unfortunate alliance with wicked King Ahab of the Northern Kingdom, he installed judges throughout the nation. He instructed these leaders to:

> *"Take heed to what you are doing, for you do not judge for man but for the LORD, who is with you in the judgment. Now therefore, let the fear of the LORD be upon you; take care and do it, for there is no iniquity with the LORD our God, no partiality, nor taking of bribes."*
> *- 2 Chronicles 19:6-7*

Further, he warned them about any offenses which come before them "against law or commandment, against statute or ordinances, you should warn them" (2 Chronicles 19:10). To judge and warn people about offenses against the law, it would be expected the people would need to know the Law. Therefore, it is reasonable to conclude his teaching program was widespread in his kingdom.

King Joash

Upon the death of King Jehoshaphat, Judah once again entered a time of idolatry, chaos, and confusion when there was a quick succession of kings. Jehoram (Jehoshaphat's son) took over the throne and promptly killed all his brothers. The nation, Edom, revolted and refused to continue to be a vassal state of Judah. The Philistines invaded, and worship of the LORD was mostly forgotten. In just a few years since Jehoram had become king, Chronicles tells us he "caused the inhabitants of Judah to commit harlotry and led Judah astray." The conditions became so ungodly the prophet Elijah sent a letter to Jehoram predicting he would succumb to a painful sickness (2 Chronicles 21:12-15). His death would seem to have been a relief as 2 Chronicles 21:20 states how his reign ended "to no one's sorrow." Clearly, there was no longer any emphasis on the teaching of the Law as there was under his father's reign.

His son, Ahaziah, was no better. Under his authority, Judah continued their downward spiral of spiritual apostasy. After reigning for just one year, his mother, Athaliah, assumed control over the nation. She was the daughter of the wicked King Ahab of the northern kingdom and may have desired to put both kingdoms under her control. She is described as a "wicked woman" (2 Chronicles 24:7) with good reason. She killed any remaining heirs of the royal family. The line of David seemed to have been snuffed out – except for one person. King Ahaziah had one son, Joash, who survived the assault on the Davidic line. Rescued by his aunt, the wife of the High Priest Jehoiada, Jehoshabeath (referred to as "Jehosheba" in 2 Kings 11:2) hid the infant son of the king, thus preserving the line of David.

While Joash is considered a good king who followed the LORD, there is no mention of the Law being taught under his reign. He did, however, "set his heart" on the repair of the temple. It is probable the high priest Jehoiada taught the Law and at least oversaw any teaching of the Law performed by priests. King Joash reigned 40 years, and for the most part, his reign was a peaceful time. Yet, as the pattern continued for many of the kings of Judah, in his later years, he drifted away from following God. He even had the son of Jehoiada executed when he confronted Joash about his apostasy.

Upon his death, the Davidic monarchy continues for a number of generations, with some kings serving the LORD to various degrees (i.e., Kings Uzziah and Amaziah), while others (King Ahaz) completely rebelling against the LORD and serving false gods with pagan rituals. It was nearly 115 years from the death of King Joash to the beginning of the reign of Hezekiah.

King Hezekiah

When Hezekiah became king after the disastrous reign of his father Ahaz, one of Hezekiah's early reforms – just as King Joash years earlier – was the restoration of the temple. In his first year on the throne, he gathered the priests and Levites and instructed them to "sanctify themselves" (2 Chronicles 29:4-5). He stated in verse 10 how "it is in my heart to make a covenant with the LORD God of Israel." The work they performed was a direct result of submitting to the words of the Law.

> *"And they gathered their brethren, sanctified themselves, and went according to the commandment of the king, **at the words of the LORD**, to cleanse the house of the LORD."*
> *– 2 Chronicles 29:15 (emphasis mine)*

Through his leadership, they once again observe Passover as a nation, making it an official part of public worship. Sometime during this process, the public teaching of the Law of God was encouraged by the king.

> *"And Hezekiah gave encouragement to all the Levites **who taught the good knowledge of the LORD;** and they ate throughout the feast seven days, offering peace offerings and making confession to the LORD God of their fathers."* - 2 Chronicles 30:22 (emphasis mine)

After the Passover was celebrated, many who were present at the celebration went to other cities of Judah and broke down the "sacred pillars." They generally removed or destroyed all pagan idols and altars (2 Chronicles 31:1). Hezekiah appointed a portion of his possessions to be used for both the morning and evening offerings (2 Chronicles 31:3).

Not only was worship restored in the temple and the pagan altars destroyed, but he saw to the support of the teaching priests so they might be able to concentrate on the law.

> *"Moreover he commanded the people who dwelt in Jerusalem to contribute support for the priests and the Levites, that they might devote themselves to the Law of the LORD."* – *2 Chronicles 31:4*

King Hezekiah had a heart for worship but he also wanted to see the Law understood and taught within the nation. His actions and attitude concerning his devotion to God are summed up in verse 21:

> *"And in every work that he began in the service of the house of God, in the law and in the commandment, to seek his God, he did it with all his heart. So he prospered."*
> *– 2 Chronicles 31:21*

This revival and renewal of serving the LORD protected Judah from the invasion of Assyria and brought peace and security to the land. Just as under Kings Jehoshaphat and Joash, when there was a priority on serving God by obeying the Law, there was peace and security in the land.

The tranquil reign of Hezekiah did not continue upon his death, however. He was succeeded by his son Manasseh which resulted in turbulent decades of apostasy and debauchery.

"And he did evil in the sight of the LORD, according to the abominations of the nations whom the LORD had cast out before the children of Israel. For he rebuilt the high places which Hezekiah his father had destroyed; he raised up altars for Baal, and made a wooden image, as Ahab king of Israel had done; and he worshiped all the host of heaven and served them." – 2 Kings 21:2-3

Manasseh's son Amon was no better, and in fact, his own servants killed him (2 Chronicles 33:24). He was replaced by Amon's son, Josiah, who, even as a young man, *"began to seek the God of his father David"* (2 Chronicles 32:3).

King Josiah
Like his great-grandfather before him, the reforms he instilled resulted in a great revival. In Josiah's case, the revival was kick-started by finding a copy of the Law within the temple as it was being repaired.

The Law had been neglected for decades, and in Manasseh's zeal to serve Baal, it is reasonable to conclude he had copies of the Law destroyed. It is also reasonable to surmise that at some point, a devoted follower of God had hidden a copy of the Law somewhere within the temple, possibly hoping to preserve it, believing it would be found during a friendlier monarch's reign.

When it was brought before the king, and the words of the law were read to him, he responded with humility. Realizing the nation had forsaken the law and, therefore, forsaken God, he gathered the nation together and had the words of the law read to them.

*"The king went up to the house of the LORD with all the men of Judah, and with him all the Inhabitants of Jerusalem—the priests and the prophets and all the people, both small and great. And **he read in their hearing all the words of the Book of the Covenant** which had been found in the house of the LORD"*. – 2 Kings 23:2

(emphasis mine)

This was a truly remarkable event. It would have been as if a church—which had drifted from using any scripture—was doing some renovations, and one day as the janitor was cleaning out some debris in the basement finds a Bible. He runs up to the Pastor's office and says, "Hey, Pastor, we were cleaning up downstairs and look what we found behind the boiler. This book looks important!" After a quick perusal by the pastor, it is decided this book needs to be read before the congregation. Upon his public reading, revival breaks out among the congregation.

Josiah stood before the people and made a public covenant with the LORD to keep the Law and to "perform the words of this covenant that were written in this book" (2 Kings 23:3). Finding an old copy of the Law, reading it, and then having it read publicly to his people, resulted in reform and revival which even surpassed the revival of Hezekiah's time. Not since the days when the Law was read on mountains of Gerizim and Ebal had the entire nation listened as the Word of God was read to them. Josiah encouraged priests in their role and recognized the importance of having teaching priests for the people (2 Chronicles 35:2-3).

Once again, Judah celebrated Passover on a grand scale – covered in detail in 2 Chronicles 35:1-19 and 2 Kings 23:21-25. Instructions about celebrating the Passover were taken directly from the Law (2 Kings 23:24, 2 Chronicles 35:6). These passages indicate how important it was to the king to follow the Law closely as they repented from the debauchery of the previous rulers.

This Passover celebration was held in the eighteenth year of his thirty-one-year reign. While little is written about the latter half of his time as king until his untimely death at the hands of Necho, King of Egypt, it seems reasonable to conclude the nation continued to celebrate Passover each year and continued to follow the precepts of the Law.

Nehemiah and Ezra
During the exile in Babylon, there was some teaching of the Law as there were prophetic voices. Jeremiah and Ezekiel wrote during those days and no doubt there were priests and teachers of the law who taught the exiles the Law of Moses, Psalms, and the prophetic books.

Upon the return of some of the exiles under the leadership of Ezra, worship is restored at Jerusalem. At this early point, the temple had yet to be rebuilt, but they did build an altar to the LORD. In Ezra 3, we read where the rebuilt altar was used to offer burnt offerings, "as it is written in the Law of Moses" (Ezra 3:2). In verse 4, they kept the Feast of Tabernacles "as it is written" and they offered daily burnt offerings.

While there isn't mentioned any direct teaching of the Law in these passages, there was knowledge of what the Law required. Someone – probably Ezra – told or reminded these people, who had not seen or experienced the previous temple or its sacrifices, of their responsibilities concerning the Law of Moses. Ezra is described as being a man dedicated to teaching the Law.

> *"For Ezra had prepared his heart to seek the Law of the LORD, and to do it, and to teach statutes and ordinances in Israel." – Ezra 7:10*

Ezra was a man who sought after God. He wanted the people to know Him through the Law and made a point to teach the Law of God to the people.

Later, when Nehemiah returns to Jerusalem, he begins a wall-building campaign. When this large project is completed, those living in the city and those in many surrounding smaller villages gathered together for a dedication service. Ezra read to the group the Law of Moses.

> *"Now all the people gathered together as one man in the open square that was in front of the Water Gate; and they told Ezra the scribe to bring the Book of the Law of Moses, which the LORD had commanded Israel."* – Nehemiah 8:1

This gathering was significant. Everyone attended, both men and women, young and old.

> *"So Ezra the priest brought the Law before the assembly of men and women and all who could hear with understanding on the first day of the seventh month."* – Nehemiah 8:2

They listened to Ezra read from the Law for a considerable length of time. Imagine this occurring in the weekly service you attend…

> *"Then he read from it in the open square that was in front of the Water Gate from morning until midday, before the men and women and those who could understand; and the ears of all the people were attentive to the Book of the Law."* – Nehemiah 8:3

How early he started reading isn't mentioned, but this event had to have occurred over a period of several hours. In verse 5, we read how the people stood this entire time. Further, in verse 8, we read where the Word was explained to them deeper – beyond just reading the Law.

> *"So they read distinctly from the book, in the Law of God; and they gave the sense, and helped them to understand the reading."* – Nehemiah 8:8

Later, the Law was read publicly every day when they celebrated the feast of Tabernacles (Nehemiah 8:18). In chapter 9, we see the same pattern as the nation assembled together reading from the Book of the Law "one-fourth of the day" (Nehemiah 9:3). The people of the returning exiles knew the importance of listening to and learning from the Law.

Conclusion

The success of ancient Israel rose and fell in direct relation to how they handled the Law, the Word of God. When their leaders made the Law a priority, the people and the nation as a whole flourished. But when the Word of God was neglected or considered irrelevant, the nation faltered.

Their successes and failures are a model for us. If we, as individuals, families, churches, and communities, wish to succeed, a priority must be the teaching of the Word of God in all human spheres. Leaders need to make the Word of God accessible to people under their care, encourage them to spend time in the Word, and directly teach from the Scriptures.

Churches and modern evangelical leaders tend to spend considerable time studying patterns of people and trying to figure out ways of making church more acceptable to the masses. A colossal number of books have been written, and many conferences have been organized trying to figure out how to make our churches more successful. While the intentions of many of those books and conference organizers is honorable, a simpler and more effective strategy might be to just encourage more churches to make the Bible a higher priority. Teaching the Bible is effective and relevant. Further, it has the backing of thousands of years of history. When the Word was made a priority and taught, the people – and the nation – flourished.

For the modern believer, one must find a church home where the teaching of the Word is a priority. It is vital to one's walk with the LORD. Sitting under wise Biblical instruction on a regular basis, paying attention, and applying what you've learned, yields irreplaceable fruit. Like Ezra, we need to make seeking, obeying, and teaching God's Word the number one priority of our spiritual lives.

> *"For Ezra had prepared his heart to seek the Law of the LORD, and to do it, and to teach statutes and ordinances in Israel." – Ezra 7:10*

Jeff Millslagle has been a Bible student and teacher for over 40 years. He is the author of 2 books and periodically teaches at City On A Hill Teaching Center. Jeff and his wife Orpha have been married for over 45 years and live in the Toledo area.

A Founding Era Sermon That Applies Today
On the Evils of a Weak Government

Excerpts from John Smalley's sermon given in Hartford, Connecticut in 1800

What John Smalley observed 224 years ago is just as poignant to our ears today. The title of his message was "On The Evils Of A Weak Government."

"One more way was hinted, in which those who govern, may weaken government; and that is, by being men of a vicious character, or by not paying a due attention to the strict regularity of their own lives. Indeed, 'a wicked ruler' is often strong, and fierce, and active, as 'a roaring lion and a ranging bear; but rarely for the benefit of the 'poor people.' He will not be eager to pluck the spoil our of the mouth of the fraudulent villain, or ethe violent oppressor, unless that he may get it into his own…when the makers or judges of laws, are themselves notorious breakers of them, or of the laws of heaven, government will necessarily fall into contempt…their example will encourage evil doers, more than all the punishments they are likely to inflict, will be a terror to them, 'The wicked walk on every side while the vilest men are exalted.'"

Pain

By Isaac Smythia

Exquisite pain! That's the name I gave to what I experienced for the first 12 hours following my ten-foot fall off a ladder onto a hard, polished stone floor in Uruguay, South America. The bones in both of my heels shattered under the direct weight of my falling body. It was like nothing that I had experienced before or since, and it began a six-month journey that saw me medevacked back to the States for the insertion of 10 screws and a plate into each of my heels. I was wheelchair-bound while my heels knit themselves together so that I could walk again.

I believe in the healing power that comes from faith in the name of Jesus Christ. My broken wrist was healed when I was 17. I had fallen from a rope swing onto my right wrist on a Saturday evening. Our family doctor set my wrist and wrapped it in a splint until the swelling went down enough to put it in a cast. But during the following Sunday evening youth service, a prophetic word declared that God had healed me. I removed the splint and believed God. The doctor talked to my mother about forcing me to get the cast, but Mom stood with me in faith. For the past 50+ years, I have not had a single problem with my wrist.

However, there is a difference between believing God for healing and denying the harsh reality of pain. Pain is God's engine light for our bodies and hearts. Your car runs low on oil, and the check engine light comes on. Your engine overheats, and the needle moves into the red zone, or a light pops on your dash. Regardless of the indicator, the message is the same: something is wrong, and you need to take action.

Look at what happens when you feel no pain. The horrible New Testament plague of leprosy is treatable now. 180,000 – 250,000 people around the world today have what is now known as Hansen's disease. It affects the skin and nerves. If left untreated, patients lose the sense of pain in their limbs. Many are unaware that the stove they touch is searingly hot or fail to notice the serious damage to their body from a knife cut. The results can be devastating, loss of noses, ears, fingers, even arms and legs.

Pain cannot be long ignored. A few months after getting back on my feet from surgery, I took my family to Niagara Falls. We walked all over the area, down a walkway that took us under a part of the falls and to some of the most spectacular vistas I have ever seen. I felt some discomfort but didn't want to ruin the time for my wife and kids, so I kept going. Discomfort turned into pain, and the pain grew worse. But I decided to just ignore it. A big mistake! I had not yet learned to listen to my pain, and as a result spent the following two days on the couch, unable to walk.

The same is true for emotional pain. The pain of losing a loved one, rejection, or deep humiliation is part of being human. The warning light that pops on in your soul is just as important as any kind of physical pain.

Several years before my fall, I officiated my mother's funeral, stuffing my own grief to minister to my family and friends gathered at my home church. I thought that I had handled everything pretty well. Two childhood friends made commitments to Jesus Christ because of "Aunt Dot's" lifelong testimony. One is a pastor today. However, a few weeks later, I did the funeral for a long-suffering saint in the church we pastored at the time. Her passing was expected, and the service was a time of memories, tears, and smiles. I was not expecting to start blubbering at the end of the service while standing at the foot of the casket as family and friends passed by. I will never forget the strange look from the deceased woman's daughter as she watched me weep. Conducting that funeral unexpectedly tapped into the deluge of feelings I had dammed up inside me weeks before. You can ignore pain for only so long.

Pain is a strict schoolmaster. It doesn't say, "You've suffered enough for today. I will let you get a good night's rest." Pain has no mercy. Its primary task is to motivate you to look for relief. I worked for ten years with Uruguayan drug addicts in our Teen Challenge, a drug rehabilitation program. Some came through the doors but soon left to return to drugs and life on the streets. But many others stayed and experienced incredible miracles in their lives. They were the ones who decided to make difficult but transformative changes in Christ to finally leave drugs. Time after time, I watched that transformation come only after those addicts could no longer endure the pain of their addiction.

Pain instructs. It teaches endurance and patience. Pain teaches humility of spirit and mind. That humility comes from realizing your weakness in the face of pain. Pain gives insight as you look for meaning in situations and places that you might never have considered before. Pain develops your character. Pain teaches dependence. I often think of Paul's words of consolation in Romans.

We also boast in tribulation, knowing that tribulation produces patience, patience produces character, and character produces hope. And hope does not disappoint because the love of God is shed abroad in our hearts by the Holy Spirit who has been given to us. (Romans 5:3-5)

Paul documented his own struggle with pain.

... a thorn was given me in the flesh, a messenger of Satan, to torment me, lest I be exalted above

measure. I asked the Lord three times that this thing might depart from me. But He said to me, "My grace is sufficient for you, for My strength is made perfect in weakness." Therefore, most gladly I will boast in my weaknesses, that the power of Christ may rest upon me. So, I take pleasure in weaknesses, in reproaches, in hardships, in persecutions, and in distresses for Christ's sake. For when I am weak, then I am strong. (2 Corinthians 12:7-10)

We don't know exactly what Paul's thorn was. Some experts say that it was a literal messenger of Satan in the form of someone who made his life miserable. Others believe that it may have been an eye problem that he made reference to in Galatians 4:15. All we know for sure is that it was a torment to him. More importantly, however, it led Paul to depend on Christ's strength in his own weakness.

Author Hannah Hurnard penned the Christian classic *Hinds Feet on High Places* many years ago. I first read the book when I was in college, long before my foot problems. The book planted a seed in me that has influenced my walk with the Lord. I have recommended it to several of the people that I have counseled. It's an allegory about Much Afraid and her journey to the Chief Shepherd's high places. Because of her crippled feet, she was given two companions named Sorrow and Suffering to help her. At each stop along her difficult path of obedience, she collected a stone from the ground as a remembrance of the lesson she had learned. At the end of her journey Much Afraid emptied her bag of memory stones to discover each had become a beautiful jewel. Each trial, each pain acquired great value, great meaning.

Pain can have meaning if we look to the Lord to give it purpose. I have often been asked for my thoughts as to why I fell and shattered my heels. I chuckle and say there are three possible reasons. "First possibility: God decided to give me a Job-like experience that would help me be more like Jesus. Second possibility: It was a Satanic attack designed to destroy or damage me as much as possible". Then I pause. "Of course, it could have simply been human stupidity that caused me to use the wrong ladder on a slick floor!"

I can laugh now because the why doesn't really matter to me so much. I thank the Lord for this amazing path that I have walked with Him, sometimes limping. If it was an attack, I rejoice that what the enemy intended for my harm has brought glory to the Lord and transformed me more into the image of Christ. And to cover any lack of wisdom on my part, I am especially careful around ladders nowadays!

I go forward for prayer for healing when opportunities come along. I know God is more than able to touch my body and remove the twenty screws and two plates I have lived with for twenty-plus years. But until God heals me on earth or in heaven … His grace is sufficient for me. His strength is made perfect in my weakness.

Isaac Smythia and his wife, Terry, have served as pastors, missionaries, teachers, church planters, builders, and international speakers for over 30 years. They were instrumental in founding a drug rehabilitation center just outside of Montevideo, Uruguay. Isaac's mission work now takes him around the world.

"Pain can have meaning if we look to the Lord to give it purpose."

Marriage Proverbs for 2024
Cultivate Strong Roots for Your Marriage

You are the guard of your marriage. Be vigilant in your watch and
allow nothing to ever come between you and your spouse.

It is not your job to fix your husband or wife. It is your job to accept them and love them as they are.
Once you are out of the way and operating in love, Jesus can grow and heal them.

Never take your marital differences or problems to someone else. Only share these things
with someone you both agree upon, someone who will offer Christ-centered counsel.

More communication does not, by itself, make a marriage better.
Communication that is motivated by the love of Jesus, is quick to listen, and filtered
through the Holy Spirit who brings health, wholeness, growth, and joy to your marriage.

Always remember the vows you spoke to your mate and to God on your wedding day so
you can fulfill them daily. They are your promises and Jesus expects us to fulfill our vows.

After being apart for the day, make it a priority to share about the day.
Sharing and listening attentively honors them.

Determine to be content with each other, always. That way in every season of life you will appreciate
the gift you have in your marriage partner and never be in a position to covet what someone else has.

If you are a willing learner, conflicts will teach you more about yourself than your partner.

The Life of a Prayer

By Vonda Hogle

"Accept my prayer as incense offered to you, and my upraised hands as an evening offering." Psalm 141:2

To be perfectly honest, I have truly wrestled with writing this article. It is not because of what God says but because every time I put something down about prayer, God deals with me about my preconceptions. These are not things that I was necessarily taught, but my own projections that I have developed throughout a lifetime of praying.

Having been raised in the Church, I have done just about every prayer model that has been developed in the last 50 years.

- ACTS (Adoration, Confession, Thanksgiving, Supplication).

- PRAY (Praise, Repent, Ask, Yield).

- HEART (Honor God, Examine your life, Ask for help, Request for others, Thank God).

- SOAP (Scripture, Observation, Application, Prayer).

- FIVE-FINGER Thumb: pray for those closest to you. Pointing finger: pray for those who guide us (teachers, mentors, doctors). Middle finger (tallest): pray for those who lead us (government, civic, business). Ring finger (weakest): pray for those who are weak (poor, sick, homeless, persecuted). Pinky (smallest, least): pray for yourself.

There is nothing wrong with any of these models, especially in teaching people to pray initially when you just don't know where to begin, but as I have matured and my relationship with God has grown deeper, I don't want to just check things off a list or feel inhibited in my conversation with Him because I feel like I am focusing too much on myself. My prayer life isn't about the to-do list or the list of needs that I have. It's about talking with Someone who really hears me, Who knows me, and Whom I can be completely honest with how I am feeling or what my true desires are.

That level of maturity in my prayer life is the goal. 1 Thessalonians 5:16-18 says, *"¹⁶ Rejoice always, ¹⁷ **pray continually**, ¹⁸ give thanks in all circumstances; for this is God's will for you in Christ Jesus."* I can rejoice about a lot of things. I can find a way to be thankful in most things,

"I can get fixated on my situation or the other relationships in my life and put a higher priority on them than what Jesus modeled for us."

but pray continually? That means that my life should be a prayer. Everything I do is a communication with God, a reflection of my relationship with Him. That is challenging because I don't feel like many of my actions, most days, are worthy of my relationship with Him.

I can get fixated on my situation or the other relationships in my life and put a higher priority on them than what Jesus modeled for us. I give Him a list of the things I want Him to do for me or provide for me, or I tell Him what to do in other people's lives. I do all of this without the courtesy of seeking Him for His purpose or plan or even timing.

When I pray, timing is really a hard thing for me to grasp. I am a latchkey kid, brought up on ramen noodles in the microwave, and have been conditioned to put a clock on things. I will give God a certain amount of time to get things done. Then, I will try to solve it or create it in my own strength. I want it to be like the Wizard of OZ, where God validates my requests then grants me whatever I want.

This past year, I learned a lot about prayer, about the life of the actual prayer itself, long after it has been uttered. The context in which I learned this lesson is why I have struggled with writing it. It's because I have seen God's long game in prayer and realized that I was able to be used by Him while He made true to His promise from James 5:16(b) *"The earnest prayer of a righteous person has great power and produces wonderful results."*

I want to be careful as I relay this story because this is my story, from my vantage point, and I think it is important to share; however, there are others involved, and it is not my place to share their parts of the story. When these things took place, they were children, but now, as adults, it is their right and responsibility to share their own stories.

In the first week of January 2010, I took a group of college students on a mission trip to Haiti. We stayed and worked in an orphanage for a week. I had traveled to many third-world countries and had been in many orphanages, so I thought that my primary job was going to be to help these students guard their hearts because I knew they would fall in love with all the kids and want to take them home, but I couldn't. I thought I was ready for the task.

As we settled in, the Haitian children were all vying for the attention of the college students, and I sat back and watched as they played soccer (football) and jumped rope with them. In my mind, I tried to imagine the circumstances that would bring children to such a place. When I looked up, I saw a Haitian girl smiling at me with the sweetest smile. She was probably 10 yards away from me and wasn't smiling at me for attention, but as odd as it sounds, I felt seen by her. At that moment, I felt God say, "You are looking around her, trying to figure things out, even with some judgment, and she is looking at you with the face of Love." I was hooked. I wanted to know this girl. She wasn't the loudest. She wasn't the shyest. She was a girl in the middle. She floated from one group of kids to another, making some of them laugh, just talking with others but showing no partiality to any of them – just a little friend to them all. I continued to observe her from a distance.

Very shortly after that, a group of boys approached me, and even though there was a language barrier, they let me know they wanted me to take pictures of them with my digital camera. As I did, one of them became very interested in how the camera worked. He was so inquisitive, so I handed him the camera and had someone interpret that I wanted him to go take pictures for me. You would have thought I gave him the keys to a Ferrari!

So, there I was. Probably 50 kids were in this orphanage, and two stole my heart while I was supposed to be the guardian of hearts and not allow this to happen. It wasn't until a day and a half later that someone noticed who I was dividing my time between and said, "You realize they are brother and sister, don't you?" I had no idea! Once someone said it, and they finally stood next to each other, there was no denying it, and God began speaking to me about adopting these kids. I found out as much of their story as I could.

I had already adopted the year before this trip. I knew that was my one-and-done. On this trip, another couple who was there felt God was telling them to adopt a different girl and had contacted a Haitian lawyer to come and begin the process. They asked me to sit in the meeting since I had previously adopted, figuring I had some experience.

I argued with God over the next few days. My prayer wasn't a list of things I wanted or needed. It was a list of why I couldn't adopt these kids. It was a legitimate list, but

God really didn't care about my excuses and continued to work on me.

As we headed for the airport on Saturday, January 7, 2010, I said to the director of the orphanage, "I don't know what God is doing (though I totally knew what God was doing), and I will keep praying about it, but I just want you to know, if anything ever happens, I want to take care of these two."

That was on Saturday. Three days later, on Tuesday, January 10, 2010, I was at McDonald's Playland talking to a friend while our kids played. I was crying, telling her I did not know what to do with all of the feelings I had about these two children when I got a phone call explaining that there had been an earthquake in Haiti. The magnitude was measured at 7.0, and the epicenter was Léogâne, the town where the orphanage was.

Over the next few days, a flurry of things happened as we tried to find out what had happened with the community we had just visited the week before. Thankfully, we found out that everyone in the orphanage was safe and unhurt. God truly did a miracle, but He was just beginning to move in this situation. When I finally got to speak to the director of the orphanage, the Help Haiti Act had been enacted, stating that if an adoption was in process before the earthquake, it would be expedited. He said to me, "When you sat in the meeting with the lawyer when you were here … we will consider that your initiation of the adoption process."

In March, I traveled to Haiti to do whatever I needed to do. I truly didn't know much about what I was doing, but I knew God was at work. Before I arrived, I found out that the kids' mother was still alive. Three years before the earthquake, she had placed them in the orphanage because she couldn't provide all they needed, and it was important to her that they were cared for and received an education. She had an older son who had spent some time in the orphanage, as well, but now was with her.

I will never forget the day she arrived at the orphanage in March to meet me. They had not told her why they had asked her to come, but when she arrived, she said that she already knew who I was because God had shown me to her in a dream. She was a very godly woman who trusted God in ways I couldn't even begin to imagine. As we talked about what a future in the United States would look like for her children, she said to me, "I have prayed for the lives of my children every day. I trust God so much that I already look to you as their mother." Humbling! I cannot imagine, even to this day, what it must have been to be in that position.

I will fast forward. The two children from the orphanage did get to come to the United States with me in June 2010. We stayed in contact with their mother with frequent phone calls. In September 2011, however, we were unable to contact her. She had gone to the Dominican Republic with a pastor and his family to do some outreach ministry for the Haitian migrant workers there. Finally, we got a call from the director of the orphanage one evening, a week before she finished a women's Bible study. She stood up to pray and collapsed from an aneurysm in her brain. She passed away three weeks later.

At the time, all I could think about was how God had honored her prayers for these two children and made a way for them to have a life in the United States. The boy, who by this time was a teenager, had some issues that were beyond my capability to manage. As a result, I was unable to adopt him. He did leave my home but stayed in the city. I was able to adopt the girl, and I truly felt as though our family was complete.

That would be a great end to the story, but God's ways are so much higher and greater than ours. One morning in October 2022, I got a call from the boy, who now is a man doing well and thriving. He asked me what I was doing that afternoon. I informed him of my busy schedule and asked why. He said that because of some recent initiatives that had been enacted, his older brother and young family, the one who stayed back with their mother, was coming to live here in the United States, and he was going to the airport to get them.

Here is where the long prayer game of God hit me like a ton of bricks. Eleven years after their mother's death, God honored her prayers – her requests and trust in Him – to see all her children living with great opportunity and provision from Him.

I know this was a long story, but here is what I hope you take away from it. Revelation 5:8 tells us that our prayers are the incense that is collected in the gold bowls before God's throne, and in His time, they are poured back out on the earth. I said that I had put a clock on God, thinking that there was an expiration date on my prayers. If I don't see an answer, or at least the answer that I want, in my timing, I assume He is not answering the prayer. God could care less about our timing!

As a matter of fact, 1 Peter 3:9 says, *"The Lord isn't really being slow about his promise, as some people think. No, he is being patient for your sake. He does not want anyone to be destroyed, but wants everyone to repent."* We have no idea the impact of our requests and what work may be done for the benefit of others as He answers and works out His perfect will in our lives – if we will trust Him.

Today, you may feel like the clock has run out on what you have trusted God for or even things you are sure He promised you. Can I encourage you, however, that He is not slow? He plays the long game even when some things are answered quickly. I can guarantee that it also has a place in what He holds for the future.

Hebrews chapter 11 is considered the Hall of Faith, but verse 13 puts perspective on it, and I would submit to you that among the names of Enoch, Noah, Abraham, and Sarah should also be Erole Gentile. "All these people died still believing what God had promised them. They did not receive what was promised, but they saw it all from a distance and welcomed it. They agreed that they were foreigners and nomads here on earth. "

Vonda is the mother to two amazing adult daughters and has had the privilege of being involved in local and international ministry. She is on staff at Keep Watch, working to see every school covered in prayer so the power and presence of God are experienced in our communities.

Quote to Inspire for 2024

The quote below is from the mouth of our sixth President, John Quincy Adams. Our nation today is being pulled in many diverse directions. Very few of these are Godly directions, and this causes a great deal of consternation in the hearts of many followers of Jesus in this nation. But these words spoken by President Adams at an event commemorating the 61st anniversary of the signing of the Declaration of Independence remind us of the true roots of this nation. They are roots found in the Bible with the intentions of our Founders to be a nation that passionately loved and served Jesus as a light to the world.

"Why is it that, next to the birthday of the Savior of the world, your most joyous and most venerated festival returns on this day.

Is it not that, in the chain of human events, the birthday of the nation is indissolubly linked with the birthday of the Savior? That it forms a leading event in the Progress of the Gospel dispensation?

It is not that the Declaration of Independence first organized the social compact on the foundation of the Redeemer's mission upon earth?

That it laid the cornerstone of human government upon the first precepts of Christianity and gave the world the first irrevocable pledge of the fulfillment of the prophesies announced directly from Heaven at the birth of the Savior and predicted by the greatest of the Hebrew prophets 600 years before."

- John Quincy Adams, July 4, 1837

How did we get so far off the path?

By Todd Hostetler

My wife and I were driving back from Florida to Ohio many years ago. I was driving, and it was about 2 in the morning. Donna was asleep, and my mind was on other things. Suddenly, I realized nothing looked familiar. I had gone about two hours in the wrong direction and was embarrassed, wondering how I had gone so far in the wrong direction. I also wondered what I could do to get back on the correct road.

I feel that same way when I look at our culture in America today. I find myself wondering how we have deviated so far from Godly principles. We are definitely going in the wrong direction, so how can we get back on the right path? It was not that long ago that almost everyone agreed on what we as a culture considered to be good and what was considered to be evil. That standard was almost universally the standards presented to us by the Word of our loving God. However, 400 years of traditional values have been reversed in only a few decades. Now, we are left to question how this happened and how we can effect change and remove the insanity of our present course.

I think most would agree that, in large part, the power behind this swerve towards acceptable immorality came from a concerted and effective effort to win the hearts of our children away from traditional values and towards a perverted perspective of what is good and what is evil. Obviously, this observation is neither new nor unique. I believe within this observation lies the direction or pathway to winning back our culture toward Biblical standards and precepts. We have to understand what they understood a generation ago. The answer is in our ability to educate our children correctly. We cannot entrust others to undertake this because they have already demonstrated their vision of our children's future. It is time for a rebirth in how we educate our children.

Where do we begin? History has already demonstrated ideas in education that changed a decaying culture and affected Western civilization for the next 500 years. This valuable lesson from the Renaissance can show us an effective way to educate, designed to make every child, Christian or not, a better citizen who learns to serve others before self.

Then, I will share an even more dramatic example from the history of Israel. Their example reveals how we, as

> *"Even though most do not perceive it, our nation is also heaving with the desperate last gasps resulting from generations of moral decay."*

believers in Jesus, can educate our children to become what Jesus intends for them to be.

Is It Time For A Repeat Of The Renaissance?

First, let us examine the example given to us from the Renaissance. When we speak about the Renaissance, we refer to a period of European history that was a burst of illumination following a period of dark cultural largesse that lasted for hundreds of years. The very word Renaissance is a French word that means "rebirth." It truly was a period of cultural, scientific, artistic, economic, and political rebirth that lasted from the 14th to the 17th century. Countless advancements occurred during the Renaissance, which are still being built upon today.

What ignited the Renaissance? The answer to that reveals the education example that could benefit us today. Different historians have different explanations of what started the Renaissance. However, one argument can be made that it was launched as a result of a specific event that took place in Florence, Italy. This episode was a brush with a disaster that left the Republic's civic leaders realizing immediate changes had to occur, or their future was in dire peril. Here is the key for our consideration today: they realized that to save their culture, change had to begin with the way they educated their children. To protect the future of their Republic, they rehabilitated the education system in Florence.

They had lived through a century of societal decay that preceded the near death of their beloved city-state. That is not dissimilar to what we have witnessed in our nation's last century. Even though most do not perceive it, our nation is also heaving with the desperate last gasps resulting from generations of moral decay. Our present societal philosophies in America are entirely opposed to our founding culture of Biblical standards and faith. Just as Florence realized they must change how they educate their children, it is time for us to recognize the time has come for us to ask the questions the Florentines were asking, "What are we teaching our children? And are we teaching them correctly?"

Rebirth in Florence

In the century leading up to the Renaissance, there was a general attitude of gloom and hopelessness throughout Florence, Italy, and most of Europe. Things had not gone well in Italian society for decades. It was as if bad things mounted up one on top of another. Ill tidings came one after another in waves of discouragement. They dealt with severe economic struggles, famines, never-ending political corruption, and, of course, the ongoing horrors and fear that resulted from outbreaks of the plague. After so much time of hardship and setbacks, there was just very little sense that things could ever be right again. This ongoing prevalence of cultural depression and universal discouragement throughout the populace resulted in a growing lack of confidence in the Church. Church had been the source of hope and comfort for centuries and had been central to everyday life for over a thousand years. It is evident from the writings of that period that Europe was choked in a miasma of gloom and despair for the future. With this worldview of hopelessness, there was a rash of apocalyptic predictions. People were so demoralized by life and anguished about their future that they seemed to just be hoping for an end to the age to escape their ongoing circumstances. We see many of these same perspectives today in our culture, making the example of Florence all the more poignant for us.

This is an overview of the spirit across Europe, and Florence was no different. So what led to Florence sparking the rebirth of culture in Europe? The 1300s had been a century of woes and agonies for the Republic of Florence. To cap things off, as they entered a new century in the 1400s, a military invasion seriously threatened them. Milan was to the north of Florence, and they were in the process of attempting to conquer all of northern Italy. In fact, they had done just that, with one singular exception. Florence remained free and independent of Milan's grip. By 1402, Florence was under siege from Milan. As the besiegement wore on, Florence ran out of food, hope, and time. It eventually became apparent to the leaders of Florence that their situation was beyond salvation. With shock, they realized their 300-year run as a Republic was over. (As we compare the situation of our nation with that of Florence, it is interesting to note the similarities in longevity as well. Our nation is fast approaching its 250th anniversary).

Then, something astonishing happened that no one could have imagined or even hoped for within those desperate walls of Florence. Deliverance came quickly, and it came quite unexpectedly when the leader of the Milanese army, Gian Galeazzo Visconti, fell victim to the bubonic plague. He was right outside the gates of Florence when he died. His untimely demise led to a quick departure from Milan's now leaderless army. While the Florentines rejoiced at the stunning turn of events that led to their liberation, they also realized they retained their freedom only because of a freak historical occurrence that would never happen again. The leaders of Florence were snapped into the realization that their culture, their way of life, was on the precipice falling. As with our own nation and culture, the creep of decay and weakness happens so slowly that it is hard to recognize it while it is overtaking you. Florences's leaders asked themselves the same questions we are grappling with. What had led them to this stagnation, and how could they change things so they would never be in this situation again?

The Failure Of Education In Florence

Our situation and Florence's have so many similarities that we should also be snapped into immediate action. There is no longer time for us to sit back and hope for the best. Like Florence, we need to respond with alacrity. While the comparisons between Florence in 1402 and the United States of America in 2024 are disconcerting, they also bring to light some of the core issues that have led us to the edge of the abyss. Our situations are indeed similar, so what did Florence determine had to be at the center of change to re-establish the strength of the Republic? Where did their transformation begin? How did it actually spark the Renaissance throughout the whole of Europe?

They began by rethinking and redesigning how they educated their children. This decision to change their education system was the flashpoint that ignited the rebirth of Florence, Italy, and all of Europe. We should learn a valuable lesson from the past and consider how we educate our children today as we examine that question with a hopeful eye to the future.

The leaders of Florence concluded they had failed to raise their children to be effective and productive members of their society. This had to change immediately, which meant overhauling their educational system. The goal was to effectively prepare each child to be a valuable asset to the city-state. They had to be trained to be creative thinkers who could guide Florence through the troubled times that would certainly come. They sought to educate each child to be a good citizen responsible to themselves and their fellow citizens.

They had failed to prepare their children to lead in the future. If their Republic was to survive, they had to prepare people to lead as good citizens. It sounds like I am speaking about what our nation needs as I chronicle this history.

The leaders of Florence believed that if they could educate their children with these objectives, they would also promote a new patriotic zeal within them. How valuable would that be for our children today? They determined that each child had to be educated in two principal doctrines;

morality or ethics and rhetoric. Ethics was vital because it would train children to learn how to address problems with a moral compass to guide their direction and decisions. Rhetoric is simply the means to communicate what you know. Expressing your ideas and beliefs in a way that others could understand them allowed you to be persuasive in your communications, be they verbal or written.

In America today, our education system has not only failed to teach ethics they have actually fostered immorality instead. This cannot be the acceptable direction for our future. Just imagine how valuable it would be for our nation's future if we educated the next generations with these two doctrines; ethics based on the principles of the Bible and rhetorical skills enabling them to effectively and persuasively communicate their Holy Spirit-inspired ideas and beliefs to others! Even if our school system refuses to teach this, it should still be the foundation of what our children receive in every Christian home. The responsibility for teaching these two disciplines to our children falls on us as the Church. If the world saw the results of children who were steeped in ethics with the rhetorical skills to communicate their beliefs, parents outside the Church would begin to crave the same advantages for their children. The teaching of ethics and morality to every child would be a giant step forward, as would the additional skill of rhetoric.

Education In Israel In Jesus' Day

The Renaissance was known as the "rebirth." Our nation was birthed in the Word of God by leaders who founded this nation on the very principles of God's Word. While we have learned a lot so far about that rebirth from the Renaissance, there is an even more powerful example for us of an educational system that we should probably give a great deal of credibility to. It is the very education system that produced Jesus. We are blessed to have ancient writings from Jewish leaders that laid out specifically how boys and girls were to be educated in the land of Israel.

Education was to begin in the local synagogue. This is where learning would take place for all Jewish people of all ages. In the synagogue, teaching from the Scripture was offered, and the expectation was that all would attend to learn the teaching of the Word. That is a great starting concept every Christian household should adopt if we hope to change our culture. It is noteworthy that children of every age sat with their parents in the synagogue to hear the Scriptures' teaching alongside their parents.

In Jewish culture, this was the beginning of education. Sadly, this is something people today do not consider as part of their children's education. Most people believe education begins in kindergarten when they send their children to the local school system. We need to adjust our thinking to realize that if we want a different kind of nation in the future based on Godly principles, we need to understand that a child's education begins in the local church every Sunday. I would also point out that the expectation in Jesus' day was that the children would sit with their parents to hear the same teaching. They were not shuttled off to listen to a children's version of the teaching from the Word. They were expected to hear and receive the same teaching of the Word as their parents. There was the expectation the Word given would not return void under any circumstances. Again, that is not the way we do things in churches today, but it is the way Jesus and His disciples were educated. There is value in critically considering the difference in the two approaches.

So, the education of every child began in the Synagogue. We would do well to consider the beginning of every child's education, the Sunday after Sunday hearing the teaching of the Word of God from today's pulpits.

Bet Sepher

The next level of education for the Jewish child in Jesus' day was the first level of education away from their parents, somewhat like what we do today with Primary Education. This level of schooling also took place in the local synagogue. It was a level of education that included boys and girls from the age of 5 through 9. There was a specific name for this level of school and education. It was called Bet Sepher, which means "House of the Scroll."

This schooling was taken very seriously. They had much higher expectations for what was learned at that age than we would typically expect. The schooling focused on learning God's Word and learning to love God's Word. Oh, that was our expectation for our children today! Because they wanted the children to learn to love the Word of God, the Rabbi teaching at the Bet Sepher school would traditionally begin the first day of school with a novel way of fostering that love. He would take honey and either apply it to the slates the children would use to learn the Scriptures or apply it directly to the children's tongues. Then, as the children began to lick the honey directly from the slate or taste the honey on their fingers and tongues, the Rabbi would speak Psalm 119:103 to them. They savored the sweetness and associated it with the words in their ears, "*How sweet are Your words to my taste, Sweeter than honey to my mouth!*"

They would also occasionally serve honey cakes or even boiled eggs inscribed with verses like Ezekiel 3:3. So the children would learn as they ate these delights, "*And He said to me, "Son of man, feed your belly, and fill your stomach with this scroll that I give you." So, I ate, and it was in my mouth like honey in sweetness.*" The imperative was to instill a love of God's Words in the mouths and then in the hearts of each child. How beautiful is that? They were training them to give priority to the scriptures above everything else in the world around them. The children were given a living example of this lifelong expectation from the Bible, *"Oh, taste and see that the LORD is good; Blessed is the man who trusts in Him!"* which was a truth from Psalm 34:8.

What is the future we hope for from this country's next generation? If we do not want them to live like the world, we must have different expectations for them. An expectation to love each word in the Bible will create a culture based on Biblical principles. That does not just happen. It takes training from the earliest age and the ongoing example that comes from adults who show their love of the Word daily. The world and the world's system of education will not teach any appreciation for the Bible. We should expect quite the opposite. Part of the change of the education of our children comes from within the home and within the church experience. The Word of God needs to be spoken boldly and clearly in church, and each home should have the Word spoken audibly so we train our children in the Bible. Our children must witness how much we savor the sweetness of the Word ourselves. Then they will as well.

Let's get back to what was taught to the children in Bet Sepher. It may surprise you, considering that each child was there between the ages of 5 and 9. In the five years boys and girls were in this school, the "House of The Scroll," they were taught the Hebrew alphabet, they were taught from the stories of the first five books of the Torah, they learned to read books themselves in both Hebrew and in Aramaic. Also, they would memorize the books of the Bible. By the time they ended their education at this level, at the age of 9 or 10, they would have entirely memorized the first five books of the Torah. Imagine a 10-year-old having memorized line by line and verse by verse the books of Genesis, Exodus, Leviticus, Numbers, and Deuteronomy!

If we are honest with ourselves, most believers today still struggle to recite even the Ten Commandments by memory. Only a select few could recite a chapter of the Bible by memory, let alone an entire book of the Bible, or five! Is it any wonder that we do not have a society that understands the first thing of morality based upon the Word of God. We need to change our individual levels of expectation for ourselves and for our children. We achieve higher expectations, and so will they.

There is one final noteworthy point about this level of education for Jewish boys and girls in the days of Jesus. The rabbis would teach these 5 to 9-year-olds not just the stories in the Bible, they would also teach the principles of the Bible reflected in those stories. In fact, they would even teach the young students about God's laws from the Leviticus book. When was the last time you found yourself seriously studying the laws laid out in Leviticus? Likely not

recently. Well, 9-year-old boys and girls throughout Judah and Galilee understood the laws as well as the principles behind those laws.

That might sound odd to us today, but listen to the Rabbi's logic behind teaching the children these laws from Leviticus. We can learn something from their reasoning and expectations. They believed that those laws were all about purity, and who is more pure than a child? So, they believed that the "pure" ones should be allowed to analyze what was pure. And the children did learn those laws. They had a level of expectancy for their children that we have never had in this nation, which is to our shame. We do not give enough credit to young minds. We do not believe they can handle the Word, so we do not expect they will understand it either. The result is that we all get exactly what we expect, which it turns out is a Biblically illiterate youth generation after generation.

By contrast, because parents in Jesus' Israel believed their children were pure and had the ability to understand purity and even analyze it, they got what they expected. By the time those children ended their years of education at Bet Sepher, they had children who loved the Word of God and treasured it. They had children that had studied purity from God's heart, and they had hearts that pursued purity. That is diametrically different than the experience of the teens in our culture, who know more about carnality than purity. Sadly, this is even true for children in the Body of Christ today.

Bet Talmud

By the time children reached age 10 they had completed their education at the House of the Scroll. Now began the time of separation between the boys and girls. At this age, the girls would remain at home to be trained by their mothers in home and family-life matters and responsibilities. Judging this system harshly from our 21st-century perspective would be anachronistic. Things were much different back then. It made sense to train the girls in these domestic matters at this early age because most of them would be married by the time they reached the age of 13. So, training in those family matters was required by that age to prepare them for their role in life.

The boys, however, moved on to the next level of education called the Bet Talmud, which means the house of learning. This was the education for the boys between the ages of 10 to 14. The goal was for the young boys to continue to memorize the remainder of the Torah, or what we would consider the Old Testament. They also began to study to understand the oral laws of the Jewish faith that had been developed over the centuries based upon those laws of Scripture.

The Expectation Of Asking Good Questions

This brings us to another lesson we can learn from their system and benefit from it as we apply it to the way we educate children today. It was at this level of education that one of the main points of emphasis was on learning to ask good questions as a means of learning. Today, we teach children by imparting information to them, and then we simply test them on that information later. However, that is not the way children were taught in ancient Israel. Then, children were taught to ask questions, good questions that would be designed to elicit more insight and understanding. They were teaching children to think about things on their own and formulate their own questions on matters. They were doing something splendid for their children, teaching them the skill of thinking for themselves. Today, we teach children to have someone else think for them, which means other people then teach children what is valuable to them, not necessarily what is in the child's best interest or the culture they are growing into.

By teaching their children to think for themselves, they became active participants in their own education as opposed to simply being instructed by someone else. The system of teaching children to ask good questions taught them how. In our culture, when a child returns home from school, we ask them, "What did you learn today?" That would not be the question asked of the children returning home in Israel after a day at Bet Talmud, the house of learning. There, the more likely query to them would be, "Did you ask good questions today?"

Teaching children to ask questions as a means of education has been an established part of Jewish culture through the centuries. This is understood by the words of Moses, who said:

"When your son asks you in time to come, saying, 'What is the meaning of the testimonies, the statutes, and the judgments which the LORD our God has commanded you?'" Deuteronomy 6:20 NKJV

Joshua also demonstrated this expectation: *"This may be a sign among you when your children ask in time to come, saying, 'What do these stones mean to you?'"* Joshua 4:6 NKJV

This technique of teaching children to think for themselves by asking good questions not only worked well for thousands of years for the Jewish people, we actually see this demonstrated in the childhood of Jesus. The Bible does not give us much information about the young life of Jesus. God, however, made sure that we knew Jesus had been trained to ask good questions as a means of learning. Remember when Jesus was 12 years old (the years He would have been in Bet Talmud, the house of learning)? Luke shares this moment when Jesus was asking good questions of the Priests at the temple.

41 His parents went to Jerusalem every year at the Feast of the Passover. 42 And when He was twelve years old, they went up to Jerusalem according to the custom of the feast. 43 When they had finished the days, as they returned, the Boy Jesus lingered behind in Jerusalem. And Joseph and His mother did not know it; 44 but supposing Him to have been in the company, they went a day's journey, and sought Him among their relatives and acquaintances. 45 So when they did not find Him, they returned to Jerusalem, seeking Him. 46 Now so it was that after three days they found Him in the temple, sitting in the midst of the teachers, both listening to them and asking them questions. 47 And all who heard Him were astonished at His understanding and answers." Luke 2:41-47 NKJV

We might believe that because of our advanced society, we have developed superior means of educating our young people today. What do you think would the outcome be if we considered teaching our children by this same method? It worked well for thousands of years, and it worked well for the young boy, Jesus. That is a pretty good example set before us.

Bet Midrash

By the age of 14, the boys had been through two levels of education, and by this time, they had also memorized the rest of the scripture. That's right! They would have memorized the entire Word of God that they had. That meant that they had put to memory over 33,000 verses of scripture. That is both stunning and humbling.

By the time the boys reached this age, only the best students would continue their education. Those who did not prove good enough students were told to return home and apply themselves to the family trade. For example, if their father was a fisherman, they would begin to learn the skills of that trade, which would be their life's focus.

Those who had displayed the academic ability to go further in their education would begin what was called Bet Midrash or the house of study. By this point, the student had memorized the entire Torah, learned all the oral laws, and now they would begin integrating, incorporating, and harmonizing these two disciplines together. It was during this time that they deepened their understanding of the Word and the law. This was vitally important to Jewish society in the days of Jesus.

If they were able to complete this level of education at Bet Midrash, they would be ready to take the final step of their education. Again, remember that this was only for the best of the best, the brightest and most gifted. Now they were to find a Rabbi, become a disciple of that Rabbi, and learn to become one themselves.

Becoming A Disciple Of The Rabbi

The student would seek out and find an established and respected Rabbi under whom they would desire to be a disciple. They would approach the Rabbi and say to him, "I want to become your disciple." Then, the Rabbi would ask questions about the potential disciple because if the Rabbi said yes, he would devote years of his life to teaching, training, and being a living example to this student. So intimate was the relationship that it often took on a more personal and complex interaction than the student would have with his own father. The Rabbi needed to know if this student was good enough, bright enough, and strong enough to endure all the way to the end.

Upon answering all of the Rabbi's questions, if the Rabbi was satisfied with the answers, the Rabbi would say, "Come and follow me." At that point, the student became a "talmid" or a disciple of the Rabbi. They followed the Rabbi, and did all that he did. He would not only learn the philosophies and teachings of the Rabbi, he would learn to become an image of the Rabbi himself. He would learn to walk like the Rabbi, eat as the Rabbi did, sleep when he slept, and even take on the very mannerisms of the Rabbi. So, to the eyes of others, he was the very image of the Rabbi.

Jesus Turned All Of This Around

With that understanding, notice that when Jesus surrounded Himself with His disciples, He did the exact opposite of all this. Yes, Jesus was also teaching His disciples to be like Him, to be an image of Him to the world. However, He did this by turning the Jewish traditions around. Traditionally, the student would seek the Rabbi and ask to become his disciple. Jesus, the Rabbi of His own disciples, asked each of those twelve men to follow Him and become His disciples.

Under the system of Judaism, only the best and brightest would become disciples of the Rabbis. Remember, if they were not good enough with schooling, they were told to return to their families and apply themselves to their family trades. Think about the disciples that Jesus chose. They were all fishermen, tax collectors, and the like. That meant that they had all been told by the religious leaders that they did not have the stuff to become disciples. Jesus did not call the ones that the world would have called to follow and become disciples. He called the average individuals the ones who are just like you and me.

Recall that when the student would ask the Rabbi if he could become his disciple if the Rabbi agreed to this undertaking, his response would be, "Come follow me." Then, the process of the Rabbi teaching the disciple his interpretations, insights, and philosophies would begin.

This teaching of his interpretations and such was called his yoke With that in mind, remember what Jesus said to us in Matthew's Gospel,

> [28] "Come to Me, all you who labor and are heavy laden, and I will give you rest. [29] Take My yoke upon you and learn from Me, for I am gentle and lowly in heart, and you will find rest for your souls. [30] For My yoke is easy and My burden is light." Matthew 11:28-30 NKJV

He has invited each of us to come to Him and be His disciples and take up His yoke as we learn from Him. What a beautiful invitation to be educated by Jesus. That is an invitation we should take seriously. He has invited you to become His disciples, and if we are willing and will take His invitation seriously, He will open up the Scriptures to you as you take His yoke. It will not be hard. It will be easy because He is the Good Teacher. He is the best teacher. Also, as we learn from Him, we are then able to become teachers ourselves.

Conclusion

We despair over the future of our nation and ponder how we can possibly reverse the trends that have led us so far from Biblical standards. We worry about what can be done. I hope the illustrations I have shared have sparked hope for the future of our culture. I also hope it also challenges each of us to change our expectations of how we educate our children. If we do not begin to make changes now, both at school and at home, we will continue down the wrong path we have been traveling on.

Florence discovered a rebirth of their culture by changing the way they educated their children. And that led to a change that affected the rest of Europe, even spawning the Renaissance that led them out of the Middle Ages. We all know how Jesus was educated, and there are lessons for us to learn by applying those Jewish education techniques to how we train our children. We would do well to learn from the past so that we can educate our children to become better citizens founded on the principles of God's Word. To emphasize this, let me share an appropriate quote concerning these things we have discussed.

"Learn from yesterday, live for today, hope for tomorrow. The important thing is to never stop questioning." - Albert Einstein.

The brilliant mind of Albert Einstein also understood the importance of asking questions to learn. Additionally, consider this quote from William Wordsworth:

"Life is divided into three terms – That which was, which is, and which will be. Let us learn from the past to profit by the present, and from the present, to live better in the future."

If we truly hope to make a difference in how we educate our children and change it for the better, the starting point lies within each of us. We are expected to become students of the Word ourselves. We have been invited to come and follow the great Rabbi Jesus, to learn from His easy yoke. When we take that role seriously, only then will we be able to become teachers of others and examples of goodness and love that will attract others to learn from the great Rabbi Jesus.

After many years in Christian Radio and sports broadcasting, Todd followed God's leading to start and pastor City on a Hill Teaching Center, Perrysburg, Ohio. He and his wife of 40+ years, Donna, reside in Grand Rapids, Ohio.